Trust

Trust

AMERICA'S BEST CHANCE

Pete Buttigieg

LIVERIGHT PUBLISHING CORPORATION

A Division of W. W. Norton & Company

Independent Publishers Since 1923

For information about permission to reproduce selections from
this book, write to Permissions, Liveright Publishing Corporation,
a division of W. W. Norton & Company, Inc.,
500 Fifth Avenue, New York, NY 10110

For information about special discounts for bulk purchases,
please contact W. W. Norton Special Sales at
specialsales@wwnorton.com or 800-233-4830

Manufacturing by LSC Communications, Harrisonburg
Book design by Lovedog Studio
Production manager: Anna Oler

ISBN 978-1-63149-877-0

Liveright Publishing Corporation
500 Fifth Avenue, New York, N.Y. 10110
www.wwnorton.com

W. W. Norton & Company Ltd.
15 Carlisle Street, London W1D 3BS

For Chasten,
whose trust changed my life.

Contents

Contents

Introduction

D RIVING SOUTH ON STATE ROAD 933, PAST A
freshly mowed green field where my high school once
stood, as I make my way home from an errand, my eye falls
on a sign marking the city limits. I chuckle when I realize
that in two terms as mayor, I never got around to having
it changed.

WELCOME TO SOUTH BEND:
BUILDING A 21ST CENTURY CITY

blares the handsomely painted board, with the name of the
new mayor under it, where mine used to be. The sign—and
a few like it on various corridors into town—was put up
under my predecessor, and it made good enough sense then:
when he took office, it was still the tail end of the twentieth
century, and invoking the century to come meant looking forward, celebrating innovation. But by the time I took
office in 2012 it aroused more of a humorous response—it
made you wonder what was taking us so long. I think that
in the eight years I served, we really did place our city, here
in the middle of so-called "flyover country," on the cut-

ting edge of innovation, and moved on from countless out-
dated practices and habits; but the crush of priorities and
urgent problems meant that we never replaced the motto
on that sign. Now, in a city I love, one that embodies all
the promise and heartache of this particular era, I wonder
if we had better leave it up, and see how it feels to contemplate the mention of our current century, ten or twenty or
forty years from now.

As of 2020, the whole idea of the twenty-first century
in America is much darker to contemplate than it was in
1999, at the turn of the millennium. We got off to a rough
start—an opening decade that kicked off with an era-
defining act of terrorism, and ended in financial collapse
and devastation for millions of households. The following
decade began with a real if unequal economic recovery,
and a sense that the country might have conquered some of
its worst racial demons with the historic election of a Black
president. But that breakthrough had a backlash, and the
backlash led to the Trump presidency. And then this, the
already dizzying third decade of the twenty-first century,
began in anguish and chaos: first with a historic impeachment that quickly became an afterthought, then a wave
of national and then global protest in the wake of police
killings of unarmed Black men and women, and simultaneously a colossally mismanaged response to a deadly global
pandemic. So far, this young century of ours has a lot of
explaining to do.

Few can doubt that these events will be remembered as
a tipping point for our country; we just can't say for sure
which way it is tipping. These circumstances have made it

daunting to write anything at all. But *Trust* is not a sweeping account of how we got here, or a full assessment of what it is to be alive and American in 2020. Volumes have been, and will be, written about that. Rather, this book is written in the spirit of what must come next. With all we have been through, we have come to a point so pivotal, so decisive, that it is nearly impossible to describe without falling into some kind of cliché. (Defining moment? Fork in the road? Critical juncture? Take your pick.) The decisions soon to be made by our society and our leaders at every level—local, state, and federal—will set the tone for a decade that is itself going to be decisive.

I believe events have primed the 2020s to be a decade that determines our future. It will be in these years that we succeed or fail in advancing racial and economic justice, in stopping the worst effects of climate change, and in repairing the standing of our country around the world. The choices we are about to make will reverberate for the balance of the century. These years will either generate a vision for a new American social democracy as wide-ranging and imaginative as the work of the New Deal and the Civil Rights Era combined, or solidify the trajectory of an American decline that would itself be the story of the century, almost certainly to the detriment of liberal democracy throughout the world.

I am hopeful. This country possesses deep reserves of courage and imagination, and I believe that it remains fully capable of great change. My own experience in office and in politics, and that of my once-disregarded city, prevent me from joining the ranks either of the cynical or of the naïve, when it comes to the American project. To love a country, as to love a person, is to love a flawed and exquisite creation, to see what is best in it, to be angry when it is not what it could be, precisely because you have seen glimmers of its greatness. Such immanent love will motivate and constrain us as we decide, in the years ahead, what must change profoundly and permanently, and what must be preserved or restored.

In the years ahead, I expect my political party, and eventually both political parties, to apply themselves toward creating this decisive change. It will require sustained energy, imagination, controversy, and hope. We will have to examine the basic definitions of words and ideas we have, often unthinkingly, thrown around our whole lives: "democracy," "equity," "freedom," "America." We will have to decide which approaches we wish to emulate from abroad, which structures we wish to dismantle from before, which strategies we wish to retrieve from our past, and which institutions we may need to fashion completely anew. For all the peril of this moment, for all the political division and racial anguish and institutional erosion, this moment is filled with possibility.

If we do meet this moment, the next decade will give rise to a range of laws, policies, schools of thought, strategies, perhaps whole disciplines, built to help re-center our national life on new and better terms. Some will fail, some will be hugely consequential. Leaders are proposing ways to include restorative justice both in individual criminal cases and in a possible process of national reckoning. Theorists are reimagining monetary economics in ways that challenge assumptions popular on both sides of the aisle, and communities are experimenting with approaches to guaranteed income. Advocates are laying out new visions in every area of life, from public safety to climate-friendly soil management. Society's understanding remains limited when it comes to our own creations of information technology, which remain in their fruitful and dangerous adolescence, but whole new fields of study and policy are emerging in the quest to better grasp their dimensions.

Taken in that context, *Trust* is a modest contribution—a signpost more than a road map. Its purpose is to suggest that we pay more attention to the central role of trust. Our country's ability to meet this moment depends not only on the wisdom of our policies or the justice of our ideals, but on our ability to cooperate to achieve anything at all. And that will largely depend on our levels of trust. I believe we face a threefold crisis of trust in this country. Americans distrust the institutions on which we depend. Increasingly we distrust one another. And the world trusts America less than perhaps it ever has. Whether we rebuild that trust will determine whether we can build a better future.

There is a large and wide-ranging popular and academic literature on the subject of trust, political, social, international, and otherwise. It ranges from psychological research to philosophical inquiry to social science analysis to business advice, and even self-help. I will not attempt to survey all of this literature in this book, though I will consult it every now and then. My approach here is more personal, and political.

What I hope to contribute with this book is a call, backed

by evidence, to pay more attention to the foundational and distinctively American role of trust in our nation's past and present; and a look at how trust can be cultivated, deepened, and, where necessary, repaired. I will argue that the demonstrated level of trustworthiness of our leaders and institutions is only one of the factors that shape whether we actually trust them. I will point to ways in which trust can be a foundation for, not just an outcome of, better policies. And I will suggest that trust is not less, but more, relevant and deserving of attention in times like ours, where various forms of credibility have been eroded, sacrificed, or even deliberately damaged.

We live in a country whose most radical founding premise was that people could be trusted to govern themselves—and that the people, trusted in this way, would produce leaders who themselves are worthy of trust. That so many Americans have been excluded from this empowered "people" only helps to prove the point: each painful and hard-fought struggle by the excluded for greater inclusion yielded a better country whenever it gained ground, making American institutions more worthy of trust than they had been before the circle of citizenship was widened. Our country's extension of rights has never been automatic, straightforward, or steady. The promise of Emancipation gave way to the racial terror that undid Reconstruction. The freedoms of, and from, religion that motivated some of the first European settlers to come here have yet to be fully felt by all in this country. Yet each time America has stepped toward actually making good on its ideals, that step has served to help vindicate the premise of reciprocal trust between democratic institutions and a more empowered people. Preferable to monarchy from the outset, the more America's political system trusted Americans, the more trustworthy the American project became, and thus the more our country came to be trusted among the nations of the world as well.

Yet here we are, uncertain of the future of the American project, and with good reason. For all the progress our country has made across the last half century in things like technology, LGBTQ+ inclusion, gender equity, and life expectancy, we have remained stagnant or fallen back when it comes to economic equality, racial justice, rates of incarceration, health equity, and social cohesion. More than fifty years after the heroic moon landing of July 1969 brought with it a sense of swift and limitless progress ahead, we seem still to be litigating the unfinished business of the sixties. Consider this comment by John W. Gardner, a member of Lyndon Johnson's cabinet, in his 1970 book about what he then perceived to be America's crisis of direction, *The Recovery of Confidence*:

> *The agenda calls for an end to discrimination. It calls for a relentless attack on poverty. It calls for major reforms in taxation and allocation of resources among federal, state and local levels. It calls for an end to our shameful tolerance of corruption and decay in state and local government. It calls for new solutions in housing, employment, education, health, pollution control, law enforcement and the administration of justice.*

Introduction

Each of these agenda items stands uncompleted and requires desperate and urgent action, exactly fifty years later. We can add to these our present-day knowledge that pollution is not only a matter of toxicity but of climate change, plus a massive rise in gun violence, and dramatic collapses in levels of social mobility and relative equality that would by some measures, in hindsight, make Gardner's time look like a high point.

We don't have another fifty years to sort this out. If present trends continue, we will be swamped by the consequences of climate inaction, democratic backsliding, racial inequity, and economic inequality. This time really must be different.

These pages, then, will ask readers to consider how much more frequently and deeply we rely on trust than we usually realize—and, indeed, how many aspects of our lives depend, like unseen clockwork, not only on the presence of trust but on the ability to take it for granted. We will consider the inequality in access to that very trust on which so much else depends. Throughout the book, I will offer accounts of the ways in which a specifically American way of trust exists, but also has been squandered, sacrificed, abused, stolen, or never properly built in the first place, leading to the reckoning of our present moment. I will point to the unique urgency of trust, even at this polarizing juncture in American history, in order to cope with the moral and political hurdles that lie ahead. And being, as I said, hopeful, I will point to some encouraging patterns that remind us how trust can be established and repaired, especially in our present context.

Introduction

Trust is an essential topic, and it deserves greater attention in our decisive moment. I hope that this look at how deeply we rely on it, as well as how it can be broken and how it can be built, will motivate readers to recognize their own potential roles in replenishing a vital, unseen, powerful, and needed resource. I believe that America's best chance rests with those who are prepared to hear a phrase like "a more trusting time" and view it, not as a wistful invocation of a bygone past, but instead as a description of the future we must now work to create.

Trust

CHAPTER ONE

The Necessity of Trust

T HE YOUNG MAN GOT OUT OF HIS VEHICLE AND approached ours with a tentative smile. He wanted me to know he wasn't out to kill anyone. And that gave me about five seconds to decide whether I could trust him.

It was a crisp, cloudless spring day in Kabul, and I was behind the wheel of a Land Cruiser, inching through morning rush hour on the way to pick up a newly arrived team member at the airport. I'd only been on the ground in Afghanistan for a few weeks, but had quickly become my small unit's go-to vehicle driver, alongside my regular duties as a liaison officer. "Military Uber," we called it.

For the most part, I looked forward to driving duty. It certainly represented a status shift from the life I'd stepped away from as mayor of a midwestern city. But in the context of the deployment, it was liberating. Life within the walls of a military base quickly grows confining, and missions of this kind gave me a chance to see something of the world between our safe zones, even if only through my windshield.

I think most Americans have trouble imagining the vibrancy of an Afghan city. Television and online imagery of war zones makes it seem as if war is the only thing going on there. We tend to picture an otherworldly landscape of forward operating bases, of isolation and desolation and constant conflict. But war zones often include cities filled with the rhythms of everyday life, with kids going to school and businesspeople rushing to appointments and men buying fruit in open-air markets. And in Kabul, those rhythms included exceptionally bad traffic jams, with cars so tightly pressed together that they often grazed each other. Yes, there was a war on, but I wasn't surrounded by Taliban fighters; for the most part, I was surrounded by ordinary people, rushing about their morning commutes through the city.

Still, a Kabul commute was different. In Afghanistan there were things you couldn't trust. The methods of warfare the Taliban employed—from suicide bombings to improvised explosive devices—meant that you couldn't know for sure who the enemy might be, or whether a normal-looking street might be rigged for carnage. The Taliban had even been known to strap suicide vests to children, which meant we couldn't trust our most basic assumptions about who was safe and who was dangerous.

So when a young man suddenly started approaching my vehicle, my life and his were instantly at risk. I had no way to be certain if he meant any harm toward me and the gunnery sergeant in the passenger seat. What I did know was that the intersection I was navigating had a nickname. The maps called it Massoud Circle, but the Marines called it "Suicide Circle." You could never be sure what was about to happen here. Indeed, a few days after I'd first arrived in-country, the officer I was relieving showed me a photo taken from inside his vehicle, while driving in this area, of a pedestrian who had walked up to the SUV, in a traffic jam just like this one, and suddenly, bizarrely, begun hacking at his window with a large knife.

But the man in front of us now was smiling—sheepishly if not nervously. He was making eye contact and gesturing toward the front of my vehicle, trying to express that he needed something from me. As best I could tell, he didn't mean harm, and yet I couldn't understand or explain his behavior. And he didn't seem to be getting the drift of my own nonverbal communication, which was intended to send the message that I needed him to stay well away from the vehicle. As the seconds passed, I had a choice: I could *trust* that the man had good intentions, or I could jump out of the lightly armored SUV in the middle of a traffic jam and level my M4 at him until he retreated.

I had been trained not to exit a vehicle outside the wire unless there was no safe alternative. A lightly armed contingent like ours did not want to be exposed on a street where we could easily be surrounded. At the same time, I also knew that the wheel well of a vehicle is a favorite place for Taliban fighters to affix magnetically attached IEDs, which could make this driver's seat the last place in Afghanistan I'd want to be. Why else would he have gotten out of his car? Why else would he be reaching toward my driver's-side front wheel?

I decided to sit tight. He didn't exactly have his hands up, but they seemed empty as far as I could discern. Getting out of the vehicle seemed to be the greater risk. Based on the partial information I had, from what I could see with my eyes and from a gut sense that we would be okay, I had decided, in the end, to *trust* him.

Then, a second later, the nerve-racking encounter was over. I watched him back away, just as gingerly as he'd approached, holding a piece of fiberglass. It turned out that a small bit of his car had gotten enmeshed in mine without my noticing, as our vehicles pressed against each other in the scrum of traffic. He wasn't out to attack anyone. He just wanted his property back—a piece of siding from his Corolla that he couldn't shrug off losing.

For days afterward, the scene played itself over, again and again, in my mind. I pictured all of the alternate endings, all of the tragic possibilities. I thought about how close I had come to pulling my gun on him, and how easy it would have been for this routine traffic encounter to escalate. I can only wonder how much fear he felt as he approached my vehicle, and just how confident *he* was in trusting *me* to reciprocate his good intentions. Most people who have pulled driving duty in Iraq or Afghanistan have a story or two about having to guess what would happen next in some otherwise mundane situation, because in a war zone, even the most basic interactions can become fraught with fear and danger. Distrust is not simply an attitude; it's a tool of self-defense.

Society works best when we can take its functions for granted. It works best when we can trust that our personal safety is never in doubt. To operate in a theater like Afghanistan is to learn the foundational importance of that kind of trust—by having to do without it for a while. I intuitively came to learn what it meant to exist in a place

I couldn't trust, routinely encountering people I couldn't trust, who, in turn, often could not be sure if they should trust me. I learned how toxic that was, how dangerous. For many, that toxicity remains after they return home from this kind of environment, affecting their health by robbing them of their habits of trust. When you can't trust anything, you have to spend your waking thoughts questioning everything. That will help you survive in a war zone, but it is no way to live.

What I came to realize is this: trust, often unseen, is indispensable for a healthy, functioning society. And in the absence of trust, nothing that works can work well.

★   ★   ★

IT'S HARD TO DESCRIBE the strangeness of running for president for more than a year and then, one day, returning to your home and attempting to gain some semblance of ordinary life. The shift is even more total if, as in my case, you have left office during the campaign and no longer have a job waiting for you. After months of nonstop motion, after the whiplash of three- or even four-state travel days, the race was run and I was home. No more speeches, debates, press conferences, Twitter dustups— no more bubble of staff, black SUVs, or small airplanes whisking me between tiny airports on the outskirts of rural communities.

And if anything can be stranger than the sudden and dramatic change of coming off a presidential campaign, it's for all that to happen at almost the same moment that the country enters a historic, nationwide emergency lockdown.

To wrap up the campaign—and also as something of a cool-down lap—my unstoppable team had planned for me to take a two-week-long tour of the country to meet with and thank supporters and urge them to join me in supporting the Biden campaign, followed by what Chasten and I hoped would be some kind of epic beach vacation, our first real respite together in a long time. (The previous August, with considerable effort, the campaign had managed to schedule a stretch of time off for us to spend together at a borrowed vacation home in California; that vacation lasted two days.) Over the years, we had accumulated a preposterous quantity of hotel points and airline miles. Now, in South Bend's chilly and cloudy March, it was finally time to use them.

But like so many other things in March of 2020, the thank-you tour was cut short, and within a couple weeks of dropping out of the race, there was literally nowhere to go. Every morning felt like Saturday, and the first pressing concern of the day was not some overnight news event I'd be asked about in a morning interview, some presidential tweet or international incident or maneuver by a competitor, but a round of insistent nuzzling by Buddy and Truman, provoking a groggy debate over who would get up first and feed the hounds.

There was, as they say, a lot to process. Our campaign hadn't gone the distance, but I was deeply proud of what we had built. A stellar team of campaign staff, volunteers, and supporters had propelled my improbable campaign to a historic win in Iowa. Our strategy of "relational organizing" had defied expectations in the early states, my emergence from obscurity had shown that you don't have to be wealthy or nationally known to mount a serious presidential campaign, and the fact of being the first openly gay candidate to win a state had touched countless lives, as Chasten and I were reminded daily by reams of mail that didn't stop coming when the campaign ended.

Of course, having come so close, it was also hard not to think about how things might have gone differently. Debate moments replayed in my mind, and I imagined how I might have answered this or that question differently, campaigned a little more in this region and less in that one, phrased this or that tweet another way. I wondered what really would have happened with the momentum in our campaign if our Iowa victory had been officially called the night it had happened, and not three weeks later.

But more than anything, I was concentrating on the miracle of being restored to everyday life—the simple relief of being home with Chasten, whom I had barely been able to see for longer than a rushed meal or an exhausted few hours together in the same hotel room between days of campaigning. Now, locked in isolation, we were spending more time together than at any time since we had met. We watched TV together nightly, discovering, as if new, the movies and shows everyone had been talking about two or three years earlier.

It didn't take long for political work to resume— mobilizing my political supporters to help Joe Biden and other candidates I believed in, forming a nonprofit and a political action committee, and weighing in on policy discussions. But the pace was radically different, travel was out of the question, and the "office" was ten paces from the bedroom.

We took the dogs on long walks as the snow receded and buds started to appear on trees, caught up on the phone with old friends, nourished neglected relationships. Chasten continued perfecting his cooking skills and started paying attention to our long-ignored lawn, while I specialized in dishwashing and laundry. And soon—inevitably, given how much time we were finally spending at home—came the housecleaning blitz.

It was in the midst of all this, puttering in a neglected corner of our attic, that I rediscovered a possession that, I admit, once meant as much to me as the whole house does now: my baseball card collection. I opened the long, sturdy white cardboard box and found rows with thousands— and I do mean thousands—of cards, meticulously alphabetized and organized into sets. Then I noticed, in one of the rows, a small blue box, an object I hadn't touched in twenty-five years, but one I had thought about often.

It came into my hands at the North Village Mall, which, like so many outposts of my Northern Indiana childhood, no longer exists. It wasn't a "mall" in the full sense, no department stores or anything like that, but more of an indoor version of a strip mall, and a frequent stop on the family errand circuit when I was little. I can't remember any of the shops, but I do remember the classic lacquered brick tile of that 1980s fashion, which lined the floor, and little fountains with the faint smell of chlorine where people would cast pennies and make anonymous wishes. But mostly I remember the day when it hosted a baseball card show that had come to town.

I was about ten years old, and by then I had built up a sizable collection, one pack at a time. Religiously consulting the published prices in *Beckett Baseball Card Monthly*, I knew everything there was to know about the rising and falling value of every notable card in my possession. In my mind, I was like a little day trader—except I was only ever buying, not selling. Other than the occasional low-stakes transaction with my friend Joe, there hadn't been many chances to see how much these cards could actually fetch. The arrival of a baseball card show meant that I finally had a chance to sell.

After persuading my mother to take me to the show, I brought a choice selection of my best cards, ready to cash out some gains. But when I got to the first traveling baseball card dealer, things didn't go as my young mind had envisioned. My head barely peeking over the top of the glass case, I watched as this man shuffled through my treasure, not looking too impressed. A cash offer wasn't going to happen, he told me. "But I can make you a trade," he said, with just a little glimmer of intrigue. And that's when he picked up a small blue box for me to behold, just a little bigger than a deck of playing cards: the 1992 Upper Deck All-Star FanFest set.

It was an extremely rare set, he confided, and he just happened to have a few of these gems, which could probably fetch him $100 or more and were sure to go up in value. This was great news! Based on the latest issue of *Beckett*,

I estimated that my cards were worth about $70. This was better than cash, I thought. I wondered why he was willing to make such a generous offer.

The cards changed hands, and I barely even tried to conceal my excitement as I walked back out to find my mom, holding this new crown jewel of my baseball card collection. Seeing me pass by, a teenager lounging on the edge of a nearby fountain caught my eye and flashed a knowing smile (a smile whose meaning was lost on me at the time). "Is that the Upper Deck All-Star FanFest set?" he asked.

"Yup!" I replied, amazed at the quick confirmation of the value of this treasure in my hands. Here was validation that these box sets really were a big deal: even this random teenager could spot one from ten paces away. How had I never heard of this remarkable collectible before? Why was it not mentioned in *Beckett*? Clearly it really was something rare and unique.

You can imagine how this story ends.

It cost me about seventy bucks' worth of good baseball cards, but that little blue box became a bundle of life lessons. I learned, among other things, that there was at least one grown man who did not consider it beneath him to bullshit a ten-year-old out of his most prized worldly possessions.

But I learned more than that. I learned that there is risk involved in deciding whom to trust. I learned that there would probably always be some cost associated with being a trusting person. In terms that would serve me well years later, in contexts ranging from economic development negotiation meetings in my mayoral office to market stalls in Tunis, I learned not to trust the person selling you something as your sole source of information about its value. And I learned a kind of skeptical wariness, about whom to let in—and how.

We have all, at some time, been harmed as a result of trusting someone we shouldn't have. And I count myself among the very fortunate that the first time this happened to me was so minor in the grand scheme of things. But from time to time I still think about that loss of innocence, which comes in one way or another for all of us. I think about the tension that exists between the necessity of trust, and the reality that people are not always trustworthy.

At the same time, as we know from a mountain of evidence, the cost of too little trust is even higher than the cost of too much. Economists comparing the economic growth of various countries have found a strong positive correlation between GDP growth and measured social trust. The effect even seems to apply when comparing different states in the U.S., with one study finding that a ten percent increase in trust translated to about a half percent increase in per capita income growth and even a positive effect on employment rates.[1] A body of evidence suggests that higher levels of trust can lower costs within teams, across firms, and throughout economies. The more trust exists in an economy or a firm, the more efficient it will generally be.

Sometimes, when it comes to speed and efficiency, a set of trusting relationships can run circles around more formal economic arrangements. In parts of Afghanistan and Pakistan, for example, large sums of money can be moved internationally in a transfer system called "hawala" that is as user-friendly as PayPal, and often cheaper, using nothing but cell phones.[2]

It works like this: An individual wanting to send money from either side of the Afghanistan/Pakistan border can bring cash to an agent, who then contacts a counterpart within reach of the intended recipient. The agents, called "hawaladars," are part of networks held together often by kinship or acquaintance, and validated by a track record that undergirds an extraordinary level of trust. Among the hawaladars, a system of ledgers often kept in simple notebooks reflects sums owed between them that they can add to or subtract from just by mutual agreement, moving large quantities of money around on paper based on a phone call and another man's word. At the destination end, for a small fee, the recipient meets a nearby hawaladar from the network and collects the cash using a password supplied to the sender.

This form of money transfer completely bypasses the traditional international banking system, and can operate more quickly and cheaply than an international wire transfer—all based on the efficiency that comes with trust.

★ ★ ★

HUMAN CAPACITY IS as limited and peculiar as it is extraordinary. We can't ordinarily remember more than a few digits or words in a row, or hear nearly as well as a dog, or detect basic deception by a stranger with any more accuracy than a coin flip.[3] But we are extremely good with patterns, and we use our grasp of patterns to make judgments, often unconsciously, at every turn.

This is one of the ways that trust comes about: By perceiving a pattern in how someone behaves, and learning what to expect from them in the future. If we think of trust as the belief that someone will do what is hoped or promised, the most basic human way to decide whether to trust that person is to notice what they have done before. To the extent that trust is about expectations, expectations are shaped by experience.

Trust, in this sense, is about predictability. We may find predictability boring in some contexts, but in others we treat it with a kind of reverence or even fondness. The relationship between predictability and trust is captured in a nice English word that has no literal equivalent in many other languages: "trusty." In some hard-to-describe way, it means something a little different than "trustworthy," yet gestures in the same direction. We are quick to apply it to any object or creature that has been repeatedly of service and thus can be relied upon: a friend, a pocketknife, or, of course, a steed.

Old Faithful, the geyser at Yellowstone National Park, can be relied on to erupt every hour or two, about twenty times a day, as it has done through war and peace, day and night, since it was first observed in the 1870s. It must say something about our fondness for predictability that this explosive geothermic artifact is named not for the fierce intensity of its power or the potentially lethal heat of its expulsions, but its regularity. As with Old Faithful, so with Old Glory: the words of our national anthem praise our flag for the simple fact of being "still there."

Cultures seek to capture the iron predictability of celestial cycles and translate it into our own practices, as if to make our less reliable human natures fit to the consistency of physics. From whatever cosmological system of worship motivated my prehistoric Maltese ancestors to align mega-lithic temple openings with the equinox, to the Jewish, Christian, and Muslim cycles of seasonal observance and formulas for daily prayer, faith practices have often had the effect of arranging us unpredictable humans, our build-ings, and our schedules, into patterns better resembling the consistencies of nature. We seem to prefer that our govern-ments do the same. The United Kingdom adorns its House of Parliament with the giant clock on Big Ben that cycles through time with immutable English regularity; by defini-tion its cycle is predictable, repeated, trust-inspiring. Going a step further than the British in electoral practice if not architecture, we Americans expect that our elections and our changes in government authority take place according to a strict and highly predictable schedule.

Of course, our moment and our recent leadership have undermined this particular source of trust. Those of us who are in the habit of sneering at predictabilities and plat-itudes have begun to long for them, at least occasionally, as a dependable output of national leaders in their symbolic roles. When the pandemic came for Britain, the Queen of England's video address circulated more widely than any-thing I'd seen her say in my lifetime. It contained a message that might be considered very obvious—the sort of speech that more or less wrote itself, with references to national character, assurances of eventual recovery, and so on—yet it was *moving* in its predictability, reassuring in contrast to an American president who could not bring himself to utter even the most basic, ritual encouragements that are supposed to be a standard work product of the presidency, no matter how reform-minded or how conservative its occupant. Among the many policy ideas and pledges I put forward on the campaign trail, few were as warmly received by crowds, from Iowa to California, as my more general promise of a presidency that could lower rather than raise Americans' blood pressure when they watched the news.

A political system like ours relies on certain kinds of consistency in order for change even to be possible. This is why it matters so much that in every presidential election we've ever had, the loser has peacefully if unhappily accepted the results. Sometimes eyes roll at the banality as cable commentators every four years mention and praise that "peaceful transition of power" while covering the rituals of inauguration, as if this were being put to the test with great uncertainty every four years. But we *need* it to be banal, to be taken for granted. And much of the mounting political unease across America in 2020 came from political and media analysts beginning to seriously question, for the first time, if a defeated president could be expected to behave as every one of his predecessors had, and leave.

* * *

EVERY DAY ON THE campaign trail could feel like an out-of-body experience, but none more so than the last day. It was Sunday, the first of March, and I had woken up in a Hampton Inn near Plains, Georgia. Here, I had begun to accept that it was time to bring things to a close. I'd been up into the early hours of the morning on the phone with staff, perched on the corner of the hotel bed with an iPad in front of me while Chasten sat nearby, my exhausted eyes trying to focus on bar charts and spreadsheets predicting delegate numbers in various scenarios after Saturday's primary in South Carolina.

After sleeping on it, it was clear as I got up that Sunday that this should be the final day of what had been a long and fulfilling campaign. We'd exceeded all expectations in a field that had at one point included more than two dozen candidates. We had prevailed in Iowa and earned a top-four finish in each of the first four states. But now the math was inescapable, and our path to victory was impossibly steep. And if my campaign was no longer viable, I had a responsibility to move quickly and do my part for party unity, knowing that we all needed to rally around the nominee who would defeat Donald Trump. It was time to step away.

Still, you don't just end a presidential campaign on a phone call. I asked the team to put together a plan that would let me announce an end to the campaign by the end of the day, and in the meantime plunged into the morning's schedule, starting with a long-planned breakfast with President Jimmy and Rosalynn Carter in Plains.

I had first met the Carters when they led a Habitat for Humanity project in our county while I was mayor, and along with my whole community I was amazed to witness their extraordinary humility and resilience. They had played their ceremonial role at various kickoff events and receptions, but during the workdays of home-building they were all business, hammer in hand.

The Carters were in their nineties, and so was the heat index, but this didn't stop them from working side by side with the thousands of the volunteers who came to the work sites each day that remarkable week. The two of them strode purposefully across their project site, holding hands, each wearing a tool belt and hard hat, and took their place to help saw and nail and measure and raise a family home into existence. From the first time I met them after they arrived, I was struck by the extraordinary openness of President Carter's expressive face, his eyes wide and attentive as if he were expecting you to tell him something revelatory, yet also warmly assured and knowing, as you might expect from someone who had not only seen but made world history.

Soon after I launched my campaign, the Carters invited Chasten and me to visit them in Plains. They received us warmly at their modest ranch house, which, the president explained, they had built with savings from "a couple of good peanut years" on their farm in the 1960s. We joined them at Maranatha Baptist Church where the president was teaching Sunday school, as he has done for decades. At the end of that visit they encouraged us to come again; now, nearly a year later, we were doing just that—on what was turning out to be the last day of the campaign.

Over eggs and fruit salad at a small dining table in a friend's house, President and Mrs. Carter were peppering me with questions about the campaign, sharing stories about the shoestring origins of his 1976 run, and discussing issues from mental health to criminal justice reform. Since I had seen him last, President Carter had broken his hip in a fall—often the beginning of a downward journey for someone his age. But the ninety-five-year-old president and brain cancer survivor now seemed none the worse for wear, relating in good humor how he had only temporarily lost the ability to speak and walk. He allowed that the physical therapy process had been unpleasant, sounding as if he were someone my age coming off a sports injury. Mrs. Carter looked just as she had at the Habitat project, serene and lively at the same time. I wondered how much the Carters' extraordinary faith played a role in their almost superhuman longevity and resilience—as far as advice on long and healthful living, all I could get out of them was the recommendation to exercise every day.

The Carters accompanied me to a community center to meet residents of the town, and then it was on to Selma, for the annual commemoration of the 1965 march across the Edmund Pettus Bridge, known as Bloody Sunday for the violent attacks on civil rights demonstrators. Almost all the Democratic candidates were on hand, locking arms with each other and with civil rights icons like the Reverend Jesse Jackson Sr. and the Reverend Al Sharpton. One key figure was missing from his usual place at the front of the procession: Congressman John Lewis, a leader of the original march, who had been severely beaten that day in 1965. Now a living legend of the civil rights movement, he would normally be leading this commemoration, but he had announced weeks earlier that he was suffering from advanced pancreatic cancer. His name was mentioned and murmured repeatedly, and I wondered if he was watching from home in Georgia. As a student I had seen him speak after receiving the Profile in Courage Award at the Kennedy Presidential Library in Boston, mesmerized as he told the story of how he and about a dozen other children found themselves physically holding a small house together as a ferocious storm threatened to pull it apart first from one direction, then from another: "And so it went, back and forth, fifteen children walking with the wind, holding that trembling house down with the weight of our small bodies."[4] I thought of the image of him at the head of this same commemorative march when I saw him on TV in 2015, standing between Michelle and Barack Obama and looking forward with the fierce gaze of someone who had looked straight ahead just like this, afraid for his life yet undeterred, fifty years before, and ever since.

The commemoration march this day in 2020 was not the same event without him. Still, the scene was extraordinary. Fraternities, sororities, high school marching bands, advocacy groups—it felt like half the state must be here in Selma. Slowly, now surrounded by thousands of participants, we walked in the symbolic footsteps of marchers who had fearlessly stepped toward the wall of deputies and state troopers who were waiting with violent intent for them on that historic day. The brutal response that had met the marchers on the other side of that bridge shocked the national conscience, with television images from Selma moving millions of previously indifferent or complacent Americans toward backing the civil rights movement—and compelling President Johnson to respond. It also cemented the credibility of the movement, forcing a nation that had not always trusted Black accounts of repression to believe their own eyes as that repression played out, ferociously, for all to see.

We pushed along, carried by the crowd, until at a certain point all movement stopped. There were so many people on all sides, covering every inch of the bridge and the road for what seemed like a mile either way, that I couldn't tell if the pause was by design or if everyone was just stuck. Then, escorted by police, a car somehow maneuvered into our midst, and Congressman Lewis himself materialized. His frame was compact under the red sweater he was wearing, but his voice remained that of a moral giant as he addressed the crowd. "I thought I was going to die on this bridge," he said. "But somehow and some way, God Almighty helped me here." There was no sound system, but his words carried widely as he urged all present to stay engaged and to participate in the elections: "We must go out and vote like we never, ever voted before."

Before his diagnosis, during a campaign trip that brought me to Atlanta, Lewis had reached out and offered to meet; when I'd sat down with him to ask his advice, simply being in his presence felt like a benediction. Now, as he addressed us on the bridge, I wondered if this would be the last time I would be in that galvanizing and fortifying presence (sadly, it was).

Trying to imagine the faith and courage that must have propelled his steps, then and now, I felt tears streaming down my face as he exhorted the crowd: "Speak up! Get in the way! Get in good trouble, necessary trouble." He vowed not to give up his efforts for justice and conveyed his trust in the power of the ballot: "We must use the vote as a nonviolent instrument, a tool, to redeem the soul of America."

For everyone gathered there, it was a stirring reminder of how our history had been shaped through political and social change. And for me it was a dose of perspective as I prepared to travel home and end the campaign that had dominated my life for the past year. This observance was a living lesson in how the current election season, and all of American politics, stood as part of a tradition shaped by the life-and-death courage of marchers like John Robert Lewis and those who had joined him on that bridge. The commitment of these activists, none of whom held any formal political power at the time, had forced the political system to pay attention to their demands—and helped America to become a democracy in ways it had until then refused.

The marchers knew better than to trust in the goodwill of the institutions they were confronting, from the county sheriff to the state of Alabama. Nor did they trust that the federal government would do the right thing unless compelled to by the urgency the marches were creating. But they had enormous trust in one another, in the strategy of nonviolent resistance, and in the moral power of their cause. And they had trust in the potential of the system to be changed, even a system that repeatedly answered their calls in bad faith.

After that 1965 confrontation in Selma, the country saw enormous advances in the expansion of voting rights and civil rights—though half a century later, America has yet to deliver anything close to racial equality. Standing an arm's length from John Lewis that sunny morning in 2020 was Stacey Abrams, whose own defeat in the 2018 Georgia governor's race took place against a backdrop of widespread voter suppression that disproportionately affected Black citizens. Abrams had contested the results, and when she stood down her campaign, she also pledged to work for fair elections, saying, "We are a mighty nation because we embedded in our national experiment the chance to fix what is broken." Today, everything depends on whether America will take that chance for reform that was built into our system.

In its ideals and principles, America's founding amounted to a radical experiment in whether the people could be trusted to do the right thing when granted great power over their own leadership—a level of trust greeted with enormous suspicion by eighteenth-century observers around the world at the time. The U.S. Constitution exists as a kind of standing claim that populations are more trustworthy than individual officeholders, a claim woven into the way our system makes the latter ultimately accountable to the former, rather than the other way around.

The elegance of democratic legitimacy is that the people, in turn, should be able to trust their institutions—just like two people in a relationship can grow to trust one another more and more deeply—reciprocating on the trust placed in them by the Constitution. At least, that's how it's supposed to work.

We continually rely on a certain baseline of trust, beginning with the rhythms of everyday life and extending all the way to our federal political system and its state and local counterparts. When we pass through a green light, we trust that the cars waiting at the red light will follow the rules. When I eat at a restaurant, I trust that the food is safe. When you sit in a movie theater, you trust that the person next to you doesn't intend you harm. At each of these turns we are placing our well-being, even our lives, at the mercy of strangers.

All of this is tolerable only because that trust is validated by experience, and because society is organized to relieve us from even thinking about it most of the time when it would otherwise be questionable. In the absence of widespread food poisoning, we can assume that our meals are safe—we don't personally inspect the kitchen, but we trust that health inspectors do. In the absence of building collapses, we assume that our homes and workplaces were built to code—not because we have checked but because we trust that someone has. The less we have to think about these forms of trust, the better able we are to go about our everyday lives.

But what happens when people cannot trust the institutions that carry out such critical functions? As mayor, I used to visit our water facility from time to time to thank the staff there. I liked to remind them how important their work was by talking about how unbearable daily life would be if residents were not free to just assume their tap water was safe—not just reliably but unconsciously. That was before the water crisis in Flint was brought to light in 2014 and showed all of America exactly what this scenario could look like, and who would be hurt.

Conversely, what happens to people when the institutions of their society don't trust them?

After all, trust is something given by others. And it is not given equitably or dispassionately.

When I walk into a store, the staff generally trusts that I'm not there to steal anything. If I were to get pulled over for speeding, the police officer would probably trust that I had no violent intentions toward him or her. And this is true not because they know me, but because they assume they do. They see my whiteness, and it's enough to make them feel relatively comfortable in the absence of some glaring reason not to. It is a fundamental aspect of white privilege—the quiet benefit of the doubt.

When I walk down the street or through a mall, I do not have to experience what civil rights lawyer Bryan Stevenson calls "the presumption of dangerousness and guilt." For those without the benefits of whiteness, this presumption can affect countless interactions every day.

It's likely Philando Castile knew he would not be safe in his car, as the police officer who would shortly kill him approached. He had been stopped by police at least forty-nine times for minor traffic violations, the bulk of which had been dismissed. He knew what it meant to be deeply distrusted or even presumed criminal, and for no good reason, by the very institutions upon which his life depended.

Racism, implicit and explicit, is America's most pernicious form of distrust. It is responsible for more death, more destruction, and more despair than any other force in American life. And that has always been true, robbing Black Americans of their social as well as physical freedoms. "It's very hard to sit at a typewriter and concentrate on that if you're afraid of the world around you," James Baldwin told the television host Dick Cavett in 1968, explaining why he found it necessary as a Black writer to leave the United States. "The years I lived in Paris did one thing for me. They released me from that particular social terror which was not the paranoia of my own mind, but a real social danger visible in the face of every cop, every boss, everybody." A half century later, Baldwin's words have a timeless quality that reflects how much in America has not yet changed.

The kinds of racism that Baldwin described—from the personal to the structural—persist today, defeating the received story line in so many history textbooks, of a segregated fifties followed by a civil rights movement that triumphed in the reform of the 1960s and formal equality thereafter. The effects of institutionalized racism are persistent, and measurable in study findings that infant mortality is higher among the children of well-off college educated Black people in America than among those of their working class, non-college-educated white counterparts. Or the study revealing that identical, fictitious résumés with names like Jamal or Taneisha were less likely to yield calls for job interviews than those with names like Meredith or Brett.[5] Or the statistics that reveal that Black

Americans use drugs at the same rates as white Americans, but get arrested on drug charges more than three times as often.

Racial patterns of distrust are expensive, as well as dangerous, for Americans of color. As a candidate for mayor, I was continually reminded how many of the residents in our city lacked a bank account. They relied on cash instead, and often turned to predatory check-cashing outfits that charge unconscionably high interest rates. Wanting to address this problem, I worked on an initiative to expand access to regular banking for those who didn't have it— only to learn more about the sources of the problem. More and more of the residents I spoke with explained that they were unbanked not because they hadn't been exposed to the mainstream financial system, but because they had.

One recent study by the New America Foundation found that checking account costs and fees are $262 higher for Latinx people and $190 higher for Black people when compared to whites.[6] Meanwhile, Black and Latinx customers have to deposit about twice as much of their paycheck, and keep twice as much in the account, in order to avoid fees, in part because minimum account balances are systematically higher in neighborhoods that aren't majority-white. These are the result of mathematical formulas that determine how much trust an institution places in a customer; and the formulas wind up systematically placing less trust in Americans of color.

This distrust is, understandably, reciprocated. Twenty-five percent of households are unbanked or underbanked in

America,[7] and nearly a third of these cite distrust of banks as a main reason they don't have accounts. After all, it requires considerable generosity—in cash as well as spirit, it turns out—to trust an institution that does not trust you.

Baldwin spoke, now over fifty years ago, of the daily pressure of trying to function in a society whose institutions were constructed to exclude, and he expressed this in terms of the trust that was unreasonably expected of him and other Black Americans. "I don't know what most white people in this country feel. But I can only conclude what they feel from the state of their institutions. . . . You want me to make an act of faith," he continued, "on some idealism which you assure me exists in America, which I have never seen."

Now confronting racism is on the national agenda more than at any moment since the civil rights movement. Fifty and sixty years on, seeing the outcry in the streets in the roiling summer of the murder of George Floyd, many white Americans have at last confronted the realization that there can be no expecting Black people to trust white-dominated systems or institutions to change on their own. At the same time, the multiracial protests revealed that more and more people understand that the burden of making change cannot be left for Black people alone to bear—especially when it is among white people and white-led organizations that so much change has to happen.

Like many white progressives, I watched events in the summer of 2020 conscious of the distrust earned by American institutions—and humbled by the reminders that even across eight years as a reform-minded mayor, I had not succeeded in dismantling the structural racial inequities that remain so profound in my own community.

The era of Trump has permitted a resurfacing of the worst forms of nakedly and avowedly racist speech and action, giving white nationalists a sense of comfort and legitimacy that had been submerged in prior years. For many white Americans, naked racism was considered a relic, confined to the black-and-white photos of the likes of Birmingham's Bull Connor, a warning from a recent but supposedly finished past. As though picking up a rock and seeing what is beneath, many are recognizing just how much of the ugliness never actually disappeared. But the summer of reckoning after the killing of George Floyd is leading to a broader awakening, a recognition that the problem of racism is not perpetuated by purposeful racists alone. It is not simply a matter of defeating the likes of the KKK or the Aryan Nation. Choices between racism and anti-racism confront each of us daily, and a racialized reality shapes white as well as Black lives at every turn. Confronting this means, for white progressives, that it is not enough to be intellectually opposed to racism. For all white Americans there is an opportunity, and obligation, to examine and change how we have benefited from structures that we may not have created, but help to reproduce anytime we are not acting to tear them down.

This is a sobering and painful message for many white Americans to internalize. Distinguishing between deliberately perpetuating racism and benefiting from racism requires a nuance we don't often enjoy in public life. I think this is why some white police officers in South Bend will no longer look me in the eye or shake my hand, ever since I said in remarks at a police department swearing-in that "all police work, and all of American life, takes place in the shadow of systemic racism, which hurts everyone and everything it touches." To many, those words would seem like an obvious statement, maybe even a platitude. But to many white officers in the room (and, I would soon learn, in the judgment of the local chapter of the Fraternal Order of Police), it was tantamount to saying that I believed each of them was deliberately racist—and therefore altogether bad. I had not found a way to prepare them for the idea that a broadly decent person, opposed in theory to racism, could also be part of a system that has had forms of anti-Blackness among its pillars for centuries.

With the benefit of hindsight, I can see roots of the same kind of defensiveness in my own responses when challenged by local activists on whether I had done enough about racial disparities in policing or racism more generally in our community. Trusting in my own good intentions, it was hard to accept that others would not be as trusting, and hard to see this as anything but an unfair suspicion of my goals—even though, in reality, so much in their experience had given them very good reason to be skeptical of what any white political leader had to say.

I have come to understand that as long as we think of anti-racism as solely the work of defeating unapologetic, knowing racists, we will not be able to see just how big the big picture is. Real change—and any real hope for a greater level of trust—requires the work of examining introspectively as well as collectively how every white person makes choices shaped by being white, in a society where whiteness is the default and therefore all too easy to overlook.

A more trusting, and trusted, society will not be available to us until white Americans—including white liberals—are prepared to acknowledge that Black people cannot be asked to work alone in delivering transformation, and, just as importantly, that intentionally racist white people are not the only ones who need to change. We need to summon a higher level of trust in the expressions of true lived experience that Black people have been asking the country at large to acknowledge, sharing the pain not only of dealing with white nationalists but everyone else who is reluctant to acknowledge being implicated in a set of racist systems and habits.

Demonstrating this level of trust is the least that the country can do. Activists and advocates from the civil rights marchers of John Lewis's generation to the Movement for Black Lives today have demonstrated a remarkable level of faith—if not in untrustworthy institutions, then in the possibility of those institutions to change when confronted with a demand. This could be a moment to build real trust, if and only if our institutions take those demands seriously; and if we can acknowledge that no one is exempt from the burden of changing this country, least of all those who have benefited most from the way things now work.

Simply to participate in the public square, as an advocate, volunteer, or voter, is to demonstrate some level of trust in the possibility of our country's institutions to solve problems, including the flaws of those institutions themselves. Whenever this trust is shown by any American who has experienced the many patterns of exclusion that persist in this country—whether because of race, national origin, language, sex, sexuality, gender identity, religion, or disability—it calls for our institutions to reciprocate by believing what they have to say and meeting their advocacy in good faith. Rickety though it is, hampered by unfair districts, voter suppression, and poor ballot access in many places, our democratic process remains the most powerful mechanism for that trust to be reciprocated. It compels authority to answer the demands of those who need authority to do better.

Trust is a necessity—personal, social, political. Patterns of trust can be felt as vividly as in an encounter between two young men in a war zone, or as unconscious and implicit as the relationship between one driver passing through a green light and the other stopping at red. We need trust in order to negotiate daily life, to participate in an economy, to engage in relationships, and to maintain a democratic society. Our very system depends on an intricate distribution of trust, and without it the basic premise of our democratic society falls apart. Yet access to trust in and by institutions, from the first days of enslavement to the present-day economy, has been deeply unequal in our country. And many of the systems and institutions we depend on have seen whatever trust they did hold erode over time. At this tender and deciding moment in the American story, here in the still-young twenty-first century, progress will depend on our ability to rebuild what has been lost, and in some places to build trust that was never there in the first place. There are many places we can turn, steps we can take, to achieve this while there remains just enough time. But first we have to consider why levels of trust have been moving in the wrong direction across our lifetimes.

CHAPTER TWO

The Loss of Trust

A N ADVERTISING EXECUTIVE WORKING WITH Brown & Williamson, the tobacco company, wrote a proposal in 1969 labeled "SMOKING AND HEALTH." The 1950s had been boom times for the tobacco industry, so much so that Americans were smoking more than four thousand cigarettes per capita by 1963.[1] Cigarettes, it seemed, had become a defining part of America's visual culture, whether in films, highway ads, or on television. Indeed, it had been a triumph of modern advertising that smoking was somehow ubiquitous and glamorous at the same time. But the industry now faced an existential threat, as large-scale studies began to emerge with evidence of what we now all know to be true: that cigarettes are deadly.

By the late 1960s, the facts were impossible to ignore. This had become a serious business problem, and the industry needed a plan "to counter the anti-cigarette forces." On the policy front, the lobbying efforts of the Tobacco Institute were going well, the memo noted. But now it was time to look beyond federal officials and directly engage the public. The memo offered a way forward—and a template for the future of how not just tobacco, but various industries and interest groups, would go on to deal with inconvenient research.

"Doubt is our product," said the memo, "since it is the best means of competing with the 'body of fact' that exists in the mind of the general public. It is also the best means for establishing a controversy."[2]

You can almost picture the cigarette smoke rising over the typewriter in the room where this memo was written, but its principles continue to reverberate into the social media age. We live with the consequences of Vladimir Putin's Russia strategically weaponizing doubt and discord to disrupt the American political system. My Millennial generation has grown up watching oil and gas companies instill doubt to question the findings of climate science, buying time against a mounting consensus. And we have even tragically come to witness well over one hundred thousand Americans dying while some of their leaders have trafficked in doubt that a deadly virus is real.

The now-infamous tobacco memo stands as one of the great artifacts in the modern history of distrust. It arrived right around the time of a high watermark in recorded levels of trust in this country, followed by a precipitous slide that has brought us to where we are now.

Our ability to trust in institutions and in one another—the ability to trust that we are subject to the same facts, even *living in the same reality*—is now endangered. A combination of causes has brought us to this point, a crisis of trust that has the potential to be paralyzing.

Of course, people in every era grow accustomed to hearing that there is something especially wrong with society in their moment. In the late 1920s, people were already debating if the radio was going to ruin American culture. By the 1950s it was jazz, and well before I was born, television. So when it comes to the collapse in trust, it may be tempting to imagine that this is just more hand-wringing, the kind of thing each generation says to the next about today being worse than yesterday, romanticizing the past as a kinder and gentler—and, of course, "more trusting"—time.

But the collapse is real, not some mirage from the imaginations of the nostalgic. It can be, and has been, measured. A 1958 survey found, for example, that seventy-three percent of Americans said they could trust the government in Washington "to do what is right always or most of the time," and the numbers actually rose in the 1960s, especially before the peak of the Vietnam War.[3] By 2019, the figure had plummeted to nineteen percent. A similar decline can be seen across a variety of institutions, from labor unions to media outlets.[4]

And it's not only institutions that Americans approach with more suspicion than before; we're also less trusting of one another. A Pew study found that seventy-one percent of Americans believe people are less confident in each other than twenty years ago.[5] General Social Survey data reveals that between 1972 and 2012, the percentage of people who say that most people can be trusted fell from forty-six percent to thirty-two percent.[6] And that was before the Trump era brought political and social trust in this country to a new low.

What started in the 1960s has metastasized in ways we have not fully come to understand. We must understand them now. This is not the result of some natural and inevitable ebb and flow, but a dramatic change over a specific period of time, for identifiable reasons. It amounts to a genuine and historic emergency, with consequences for every part of American life. And the better we can understand the toxic roots of this crisis, the better chance we have of addressing it.

★ ★ ★

ON JUNE 13, 1971, the *New York Times* began printing excerpts of leaked documents that revealed details of America's military involvement in Vietnam. The Pentagon Papers, as they became known, did more than just explain the failures of the war effort to that point. They revealed that the Johnson and Nixon administrations had been dishonest about the origins and conduct of the war. Americans had been misled, not just about how the conflict had escalated and how it was going for the United States, but even *where* warfare was taking place. The American people learned from the leaked documents, not from their leaders, a full picture of how the conflict had expanded to include horrific bombing campaigns over Laos and Cambodia.

The Papers' contents were damning, as was the concerted effort to try to suppress them. They amounted to clear proof of dishonesty at the highest levels of the government, from the presidency on down. It was a serious blow to the perceived integrity of the White House, made worse by the refusal of the administration to confront its failures. Yet the war continued, and so did the damage.

The blow to American trust in Washington was twofold. The official dishonesty revealed by the Papers amounted to a failure of integrity, which sat atop a more basic failure of competence. In the post–World War II era, the military had been revered and admired not just for the values that surrounded service but because of a sense of achievement and competence, cemented by the victories of the Greatest Generation. Now Americans were losing faith in military's ability both to execute and to tell the truth. And because the war effort had been run by the so-called "best and brightest," including brilliant men with sterling Ivy League pedigrees originally recruited to Washington by President Kennedy, these failures even served to undermine the credibility of expertise itself.

Within two years of the publication of the Pentagon Papers, the Watergate hearings began, striking again at the question of integrity at the highest levels. Then, in an unrelated scandal, Vice President Spiro Agnew, known largely for his alliterative jabs at "nattering nabobs of negativity," and "hysterical hypochondriacs of history," resigned after an almost cartoonish show of corruption that included receiving cash bribes in his office. By the time Nixon himself resigned in August of 1974, America's relationship to the presidency would never be the same.

In some ways, especially compared with the experience of the Trump impeachment trial of 2020, the outcome of Watergate actually reflects well on American institutions—at least in terms of its system of checks and balances. After all, the most powerful official in America, the president himself, was forced from office after bipartisan congressional hearings exposed the scope of his wrongdoing. He stood down even before an impeachment trial took place, resigning to preempt the inevitable, as members of his own Republican Party joined Democrats in denouncing the corruption that had been uncovered. In that sense, at least, the system worked as designed.

But for the American people, this episode was anything but confidence-building. And the entire spectacle tarnished the public's perception, not just of Nixon or of the presidency, but of government itself. By design, the powers of American government are distributed in an intricate and complex fashion. Power is shared widely, not just across the three federal branches, but between the federal government and state and local authorities. We learn this in school. Yet for all that, it remains the case that in our imaginations, the presidency represents the government itself. Nixon's dishonesty and presidential corruption tainted everything the presidency touched, and everything it represented. And so that stain on the most visible government institution in American life became a stain on politics itself—a crushing blow to political trust that reverberated for decades.

The response to Watergate propelled Georgia Governor Jimmy Carter, a Washington outsider and Navy veteran who radiated honesty, into the presidency. And the memory of a corrupt and paranoid Nixon White House was still fresh when Carter's White House gave way to Ronald Reagan, a familiar and trusted face long before his political rise began, thanks to a storied acting career (which, looking back, includes a disconcerting number of cigarette ads).

Reagan's sunny and confident style seemed to promise a steady, reassuring, and trustworthy presence in the Oval Office as he won the 1980 election in a landslide. But if Reagan's demeanor and familiarity led many Americans to trust *him*, his ideology meant that the 1980s would not be a decade of building trust. In fact, this decade saw a new level of effort, even presidential effort, to sow doubt across America in some of our most important institutions.

President Reagan had arrived in the White House not only as a Republican leader but as the leading proponent of a conservative ideology that did not trust government, the press, or labor unions to make Americans' lives better. Riding a wave of corporate support, Reagan also brought to the White House a "supply-side" economic philosophy that had previously been considered fringe, and has since been debunked in practice, but was about to enjoy a heyday.

Part of the economic thinking that came to the White House was the idea that corporations were responsible to no one but their shareholders, that the best thing they could do for America was to maximize their own profits, which would then "trickle down" to everyone else in the economy as a matter of course. In this worldview, things like the regulations that establish companies' responsibilities to the community or the environment were seen as an inefficiency—a nuisance to be minimized.

The labor unions were seen as a nuisance, too, or, worse, a threat, and one of Reagan's first major acts as president was to make clear his view of organized labor by firing over eleven thousand striking air traffic controllers in August 1981. Previous administrations of both parties, in contrast, had recognized unions as an important source not only of economic power but of belonging and social capital in communities and across the economy—indeed, Reagan had been a union president himself, leading the Screen Actors Guild in the late 1940s and 1950s. But now unions represented an obstacle to the president's philosophy and agenda; undermining them was a priority.

At the time, one in every five private sector workers was a union member. So the Reagan administration, along with its corporate allies, began a concerted effort to weaken the power of unions, and, perhaps most profoundly, to destroy the trust and credibility that they had built up with the men and women who relied on their protection for decent wages, job security, and medical care.

Of course, what began with Reagan didn't end there. The work of undercutting unions, which were once seen as so essential in the balance of the American social contract, has continued unabated for forty years. Often this effort deployed a strategy of discrediting labor organizations, working to undermine workers' trust in the very concept that unions existed for the benefit of their employees. In 2014, the *Huffington Post* published leaked audio from employer-led anti-union meetings that took place at a number of major American companies.

At Coca-Cola, a representative for management told workers who were considering organizing, "They may claim they want to represent you, and give you a voice in the workplace, but at least my experience is at the end of the day it's all about money."

At Staples, employees were told that "unions can pit associates against each other," and, "Don't be fooled: Unions are first and foremost a business."

At FedEx, workers were advised against organizing as well. "We don't think it's good for you or your families."[7]

Frontal efforts to bust and block union organizing continue, but the most sophisticated usually work in this more subtle way—urging workers to trust their management more than the unions that seek to represent them.

By the 1980s, an alliance of industry interests and political ideologies was finding new ways to shape the political process, too, as regulations on political spending fell away. The spirit of reform in 1974 had led Congress to pass a number of restrictions on campaign spending and advertising, including limiting contributions and expenditures, providing for public financing of campaigns, establishing new disclosure rules, and creating the Federal Election Commission. But just two years later, many of the provisions of federal campaign finance law were ruled unconstitutional in the Supreme Court decision of *Buckley v. Valeo*, which largely held that campaign spending was a form of political speech protected by the First Amendment. The result was to open the floodgates for money in politics. If industry interests saw value in sowing doubt, they now had wide latitude to do so through political as well as marketing campaign spending.

At the same time, Reagan saw ideological advantage in stoking doubts about the very role of government itself. The less people trusted government, the more likely they would back his efforts to dismantle the programs and regulations that Reagan's conservative movement so deeply opposed. Of course, skepticism about government leaders was not new—and not always unjustified, especially in light of Watergate. But this was a broader attack on the concept of government itself. Still more remarkable about the Reagan administration was the paradox that those seeking to discredit the government were running it at the same time.

Reagan's famous declaration that "government is not the solution to our problem; government is the problem" came not in some campaign appearance, but in his inaugural address—in other words, the ceremony in which he was taking charge of the very government he was denouncing. His later quip that "the most terrifying words in the English language" were "I'm from the government and I'm here to help" came at a presidential news conference in 1986. By this time, he had been leading that same government for years.

As those in charge of government came to spend more rhetorical energy denouncing it than improving it, trust was certain to fall further. This rhetoric, which would have seemed alien to both parties just a couple of decades earlier, became a new baseline. Denunciations, not of a particular administration but of the very possibility of government serving people well, increasingly went from being provocative to commonplace and eventually obligatory. By the 1990s even Democrats spoke of government with skepticism. It was Democratic President Bill Clinton, after all, who declared, "The era of big government is over," at his 1996 State of the Union Address.

That same year, in the midst of so much swirling distrust, Fox News and MSNBC were born, joining CNN in the category of cable news. Their arrival continued a process that diluted the power of the three national television networks, whose nightly news broadcasts had established a level of trust reflected in the calm authority of Walter Cronkite's sign-off: "And that's the way it is."

It wouldn't take long before Fox's Roger Ailes realized he could build a big audience—and big profits—by exploiting the wariness and secret fears of his viewers. He played to their resentments, sowed a growing hostility toward government, toward immigrants, toward anyone named Clinton, and saw the bottom line grow at each turn. Offering undisguisedly ideological commentary under the slogan "Fair and Balanced," the network's hosts started referring to the "mainstream media" as part of the problem, as though a corporate giant like Fox were some kind of grassroots resistance.

The Fox opinion hosts abandoned the classic television journalist's role of seeking to provide authoritative, carefully reported truth, which had been the North Star of network news coverage for decades, and instead trafficked in doubt and suspicion. In this sense, Ailes recognized what the purveyors of conspiracy theories often do: that by playing to an audience's distrust of others, you can more quickly secure their trust in you. Getting people to trust you through consistent, hard-won credibility is difficult and time-consuming. But a shortcut to gaining trust is to simply ask people to join you in distrusting someone else. This kind of trust through mutual suspicion may be cheaper and shallower, destined to appeal only to a minority of Americans. But the lucrative logic of opinion media is that whoever you do capture in this way will become less and less willing to hear outside voices, and more and more dependent on yours.

CNN, too, benefited from the magnetic attraction of viewer eyeballs toward controversy, but in a different way. Programs like *Crossfire* presented opposing viewpoints in real time, putting liberal and conservative hosts together for energetic commentary that was exciting, if sometimes aggravating, to watch. The show built on a tradition of debate that went back to the earliest days of television and could often be edifying, but it was now increasingly taking on the character of a kind of sport. The show's intro presented its commentators in almost gladiatorial fashion: "On the left . . . Begala. . . . On the right . . . Carlson!" (Years later, I would glance at a TV while brushing my teeth in a hotel room and see my own face flash on the screen as part of a debate promo, with a low voice firing off my name and that of the other Democrats as if promoting a ten-way boxing match, and wonder just how much further this style can go.)

Because it aired opposing views at the same time, this approach had a kind of integrity that Fox News and right-wing radio lacked. But it also suffered from a built-in fairness problem that, ironically, stems from its effort to be evenhanded. Like our two-party system, a two-sided TV debate can make it seem like only two viewpoints are valid. And it implies that they are equally valid, even when one side has been thoroughly discredited on the facts. The result is to institutionalize false equivalence—in ways that now permeate our media environment and political system.

On climate change, for example, the clear trajectory of research and science through the 1990s was toward an increasingly overwhelming consensus. But to follow the "both sides"–style debates of the time on television was to believe this remained an evenhanded controversy. Eager to seem fair, networks wouldn't just invite a climate scientist to relay the sobering facts, or two climate scientists with different angles from within the growing overall consensus. They'd invite a "global warming skeptic," too, usually one funded by the oil and gas industry. As with the tobacco industry's stalling, the mission of the denier was accomplished even if he convinced no one; the point was not to prove anything with certainty but to elevate the general level of doubt (and, of course, to entertain at the same time).

Even the terminology of "climate skepticism" deserves attention for the effect it has on our sense of confidence. Something about the word "skeptic" connotes someone not easily persuaded, peering over reading glasses dispassionately and surveying the evidence. To be skeptical, as the word hits us, is to be intelligently distrustful, nobly unwilling to get caught up in the feverish enthusiasms of the moment. But there is nothing intelligent or noble about a stubborn refusal to acknowledge a mounting fact base— especially when that refusal is motivated by material gain. As climate change effects have gone from a theory to a prediction to an observation, the moral weight of this refusal has grown to an intolerable level. Extreme impacts have been recorded from coastal regions to deserts around the world; in my own inland city I have seen waters rise twice, in two years, to flood levels that are supposed to come along once or twice in a millennium. The relationships between any individual weather event and overall climate patterns are sometimes uncertain, but the baseline warming and its causes are not. At a certain point, we must be willing to call denial what it is. We do not speak of "Holocaust skeptics."

In the end, these overwrought attempts at evenhandedness actually served to distort the truth—and Americans' access to it. By lending equal credence to either side of a controversy, they signaled that the controversy was legitimate and created the perception for viewers that knowable and established facts are, themselves, open for debate. Media outlets often did this while trying to avoid a choice between two sides. But presenting a settled question as up for debate is itself a choice. And the consequence of this choice is that the debate can never advance toward a healthier and necessary argument: a constructive controversy over what to do next.

This can also undercut trust in institutions themselves. If I am led to believe that something like climate science is a fifty-fifty debate, and I happen to also notice that academic scientists are unified on the basic questions by a ratio more like ninety-nine-to-one, then the entire scientific community appears reduced to being one half of a valid debate. The very place where we would look to settle a question (at least, a scientific question) becomes suspect, and our grasp on any kind of certainty weakens. (As we'll see later, malicious actors in the Internet age would find new ways to deliberately exploit the damage that fifty-fifty messaging can do when applied to consensus issues, like the safety and effectiveness of vaccines.)

Alongside these changes in the media environment, another strong pattern developed that would inevitably affect social and political trust: a sharp rise in economic inequality in America.

By the 1980s, the basic economic bargain that had defined the twentieth-century American economic system was swiftly eroding, with rising inequality that represented a major change from the decades that had come before. In income and in wealth, our country had not only grown dramatically since the Depression, but it also had grown more equal. In fact, charts showing most measures of American inequality over the last 150 years have a pronounced U or V shape to them, with inequality very high in the Gilded Age of the 1880s, falling steadily through the 1960s, then rising again into today's period, returning to levels not seen for more than a hundred years. Today the richest one percent of American households own more wealth than the bottom ninety percent. And this kind of inequality, especially in a society built on the ideal of widespread opportunity, is simply not compatible with high levels of trust.

This didn't just happen, of course. It was the result of policies, decisions—like reductions in the power of unions, a lowering of the real value of the minimum wage, and tax policy changes like cuts in capital gains taxes, reduced top tax rates, and a proliferation of loopholes to make the system less and less progressive. The great irony is that this inequality, which largely came from decisions to suppress the role of government in supporting workers and families, has led to still more distrust of government. After all, we expect government not only to deliver services but to create a general climate of prosperity and establish a baseline of fairness. To see middle-class wages stagnate and real minimum wages fall, through years of enormous economic growth, is to witness a policy failure. And in this sense, the Reagan-era belief that government could not be trusted to do a good job became a self-fulfilling prophecy.

The rise in glaring inequality inevitably fuels resentment and distrust—not just of the government that failed to prevent it, but of any people or places that seem to benefit from this growing gap. Even when it's not obvious exactly who that is, a level of mounting frustration simmers among people who sense that their being economically stuck is connected to others making out like never before.

We can see evidence of this frustration in the way that the term "establishment" has grown to be a staple of political rhetoric—another pattern that seems to have first started in the 1960s and accelerated through today. No one can precisely define what the establishment is, but it is certainly the rhetorical enemy of every politician. Sometimes this reaches eyebrow-raising proportions, as lifelong millionaires or decades-long incumbents insist on their outsider credentials. Thus Governor John Kasich, after a distinguished twenty-six years in public office plus an eight-year stint as a corporate director and investment banker, was obliged in the 2016 Republican presidential primary to declare: "It's pretty hard to label me as an establishment figure, because I've always fought the establishment." In that crowded field, only Jeb Bush gave up any pretense of distance from the establishment, saying of the label, "Fine, I'll take it." You might imagine that he had no choice, as the son of one president and the brother of another. But to think he had to confess this status would be to lack imagination, now that we know whose "anti-establishment" campaign beat Bush, Kasich, and all the others: that of a billionaire, not self-made but born into tremendous wealth, who lived in a building named after himself and had been photographed with just about every major American political figure of his lifetime.

The same dynamic has played out on my side of the aisle, of course, where no level of time spent in Washington, educational pedigree, or personal wealth would prevent a Democratic office-seeker from at least trying to push off rhetorically from the establishment. Every politician has to run at as much distance as possible from the establishment he or she is inevitably either part of or seeking to enter, because the frustration among Americans is so deep toward anyone and everything that benefits from the yawning chasm of inequality that the establishment seems always to reinforce.

And the inequality is not just dramatic, it's increasingly entrenched. It has grown harder and harder for Americans born low-income to come out on top, or even make it to the middle, a fact that corrodes trust in the very basis of the American dream. So long as our institutions perpetuate this, distrust will grow.

Trust

OF COURSE, we cannot assess what has happened to trust across the last several decades without also considering how radically our relationship with information itself has changed. In the same way that my grandparents talked about ration cards in Indiana and air raids in Malta, I will one day talk to my grandchildren about the CDs that used to come in the mail every month or two, promising ten free hours of Internet time with AOL.

After coming to rely on Internet connections at the university where they worked, my parents finally agreed we should get it at home, sometime in the mid-nineties, around when I was entering middle school. A miraculous modem appeared, wired into the phone jack next to the big gray Mac in the front room, with a sequence of about ten little LED lights from top to bottom. To dial up was like watching a rocket launch: first the top light was on, then the second . . . then came the sound of the modem talking to whatever it was talking to . . . sounding like an Atari game's parody of birdsong or of a clarinet solo, pinging and ponging as more and more of the little lights came on, blinking and then steady, orange and then green . . . the sound building to a crescendo that recalled the noise of TV static, as machines confided who-knows-what secret binary handshakes between them while I listened. Then came a key change. Then the pitch of the static pulse tweaked, now higher, now lower, and then, gloriously, the final light went to green and I was online, in orbit: cyberspace.

The connection to the rest of the world was precious,

expensive. A countdown clock told you how many of your hours remained that month, and you'd pay by the minute if you went over. And it was tenuous: if someone picked up the phone in the house, they would be rewarded with the screech of the modem in their ear, while you would lose your connection and have to start the blast-off sequence all over again.

There weren't a lot of websites to visit anyway; I remember an online encyclopedia that was somewhat useful for doing homework but actually far inferior to the authoritative, leather-bound volumes of our edition of *Encyclopædia Britannica,* complete with that intimidating "æ" in its name, which my father had purchased used, with great ceremony and at great expense, years earlier. Often in those early years of the 1990s, the Internet felt more like a curiosity—and a means of contacting my middle school friends, Joe or Monica or Ben or Bridget, typing out confidences in Instant Messenger and crafting witty "away messages" that might be compared, in hindsight, to tweets.

It wasn't a long process for the Internet to go from reshaping homework assignments and middle school gossip, to swiftly and profoundly changing everyone's relationship with our sources of news and information—and therefore, inevitably, our politics. Internet technology held the promise of democratizing knowledge, bypassing the mediators and ensuring that the venality of editors and governments (in other words, the establishment) could not prevent the truth from emerging.

Some early observers were positively utopian. A 1997 piece in *Wired* magazine gushed about digital communities of interest in ways that look heartbreakingly ironic twenty years later: "Where conventional politics is suffused with ideology, the digital world is obsessed with facts. . . . The Digital Nation points the way toward a more rational, less dogmatic approach to politics."[8] If only this had been the result.

Still, early in the Internet age, the empowerment of campaigns that thrived on online organizing did seem to validate the promise of political empowerment through technology. Fresh off Howard Dean's exhilarating progressive campaign, his former campaign manager Joe Trippi said in 2005, "The Internet is the most democratizing innovation we've ever seen, more so even than the printing press."[9]

Other early predictions about Internet technology would be realized decades later, but in ways that the futurists might not have guessed. When RAND Corporation scholar Christopher Kedzie said in 1995 that "information revolution technologies empower citizens anywhere to broadcast charges that their own governments have violated inalienable human rights," he probably had in mind places like the former Soviet republics where he had been a researcher.[10] But his description anticipated the role that smartphones would play right here in the United States, documenting killings by police and other civil rights violations, while social media made it possible for them to circulate. The rise in social media and digital distribution of information has also meant that citizens can much more readily check to see what our institutions are doing, from the level of individual police officers to that of campaign contributions or congressional proceedings.

The various patterns of democratization and division brought about through technology are still developing. But one pattern has proven to be dangerously consistent: companies create new technologies and new platforms, and then, in short order, someone figures out how to weaponize them.

In our era, that of the toxic tweet, it's easy to forget that during the 2008 election the most potent digital tool of disinformation was the "email forward." Instantaneous and free of charge, a repeatedly forwarded email would blast out from the inbox of a politically minded uncle or coworker to a dozen semi-willing recipients, propagating exponentially in a fashion that the writers of its primitive ancestor, the chain letter, could never have dreamed of. Then–Senator Obama and his campaign team spent a great deal of time knocking down widely circulated falsities— that he was born in Kenya, that he was a Muslim, that he had attended a madrassa in Indonesia. Even his opponent, John McCain, had to correct falsehoods about Obama that came his way from a voter in a town hall appearance. Social media was in its infancy, but misinformation was already going viral.

These emails hinted at what such platforms might do to politics, even during a time when social media itself at first seemed like a benevolent force in political organizing. The Obama campaign in 2008 harnessed social networking with the creation of my.BarackObama.com, linking volunteers and organizers not just with the campaign but also with each other. The feel was one of community-building, knitting together the like-minded to build social capital.

It took just two election cycles for malicious actors to figure out how to weaponize these same kinds of platforms, with devastating effect.

As social media companies matured, they mastered the formula for profit maximization: keeping our eyes on their platforms for as long as possible. Our eyes fell, as human eyes do, on the things that most seize our attention—the weird story, the outrageous revelation, or sometimes just the pretty picture. Without any one person deciding this should happen, the platforms came to favor whatever seduced our attention the most. Some patterns of attention-getting were as old as advertising itself: bright colors, famous faces, sex appeal. But one proved to be more effective than anything else: controversy.

A 2017 Pew Research study evaluated the patterns in tone and language across various social media posts, trying to determine which emotional styles generated the most attention. The study found that posts that exhibited "indignant disagreement" earned double the engagement of other content on Facebook.[11] And so the algorithms kept feeding us the content we craved. (Not necessarily the content any one of us would consciously say we want to dominate our news media, but the content we actually clicked on and responded to—sometimes a cat video, often a Trump tweet—the revealed instantaneous preferences of our least conscious selves.)

In catering to those cravings, the algorithms themselves became radicalizing. They started to filter us into tribes and feed us increasingly vivid claims, the kind that spark controversy, intrigue, and, above all, the coveted chance to go "viral." By the logic of social media, to go viral is an achievement, a triumph, even; the term entered our vocabulary so swiftly and comfortably that we rarely pause to consider what the metaphor of a fast-spreading disease might be telling us.

The algorithms did not need help from anyone in an editorial role—speed and spread were the coin of the realm, so why slow them down with something as pedantic as a human being trying to make decisions about what readers needed to know or who was credible? And without a moderator or an editor, these spaces called forth an echo chamber—of rumor, invention, and superstition.

Fake news is nothing new. The expression that "a lie can get halfway around the world while the truth is still tying its shoes" is credited to Mark Twain, but its origins predate the invention of the telegraph. What's new are the ways the Internet makes it uniquely hard to keep up with the myriad (and growing) number of ways people can deceive you. Every new form of advertising—from the handbill to the billboard to the TV commercial—eventually forces us to become more sophisticated in deciding what to believe. Just as my generation learned to be savvy about television ads, and our elders made a saying of the idea "not to believe everything you read," we get smarter about these things, one generation and one informational format at a time. But the learning curve is steep, and when it comes to separating fact from rumor online, we're still not very good at it.

The "wisdom of crowds" can help people identify misleading information and collectively find the truth, as the relative (though imperfect) accuracy of Wikipedia demonstrates. But it is far from a comprehensive approach. Wild claims can go viral; statements of correction rarely do. A certain amount of leakage comes with even the most thorough debunking of an easily refuted tweet. A post-election poll in 2016 found, for example, that a quarter *of Obama supporters* believed at least one of three blatantly fake news stories: that Hillary Clinton was seriously ill; that she had approved arms sales to ISIS; or that the pope had endorsed Donald Trump. Those who did believe these things were half as likely to vote for her as those who didn't.[12] In an election that was decided by fewer than forty thousand votes, any number of things could be said to have tipped the scale; fake news was clearly one of them.

Today's information climate in many ways actually makes us more reliant on real journalism than ever. We may not need as many intrepid reporters to go into as many places, now that cell phone video lets people report from anywhere. But we still rely on honest and courageous reporting and editorial work to investigate, to corroborate, and to amplify. And we need reporters and editors who will not only pick up good information sourced from ordinary people, but also check on claims and content sourced from powerful people—to let us know what holds up.

Sadly, the very same Internet platforms that have shown us the need for good and balanced journalism have also demolished that journalism's revenue, with newsrooms thinning and news outlets closing at a fast and frightening clip. Between 2004 and 2019, two thousand newspapers— one in every five—disappeared in the United States, leaving more than two hundred U.S. counties without a local paper.[13] Like any mayor, when I was in office, I had the occasional grumpy phone call with editors at the local paper that covered me. But I could place those calls because I knew that if I could convincingly point to anything unfair or inaccurate in the coverage, the editors could be trusted to care. And their coverage mattered because readers trusted that the paper offered a thorough account of what was happening in the community.

Old-timers tell me that the *South Bend Tribune* used to have over a hundred pages every day; lately, the front news section usually has eight, much of it from wire services. Yet without the truth-seeking work of local news media it would have been impossible for residents to hold me and other officials accountable from a widely informed position—or for me to access a professional, comprehensively sourced, outside look at the goings-on in my own community or even my own administration. We will always need editors, journalists, and fact-checkers. And that means we will need to figure out a way to reward a carefully sourced news story with at least as much revenue as a Macedonian teenager's website can get by running a fake news post claiming that Britney Spears has been eaten by alligators. That's not just a question of policy; it's a question of whether we, as news consumers, can be trusted to click first on what we most need to know.

★ ★ ★

IF THERE REMAINS any doubt about the importance of social trust to our country's strength, just consider how much work our adversaries have put into attacking it. Americans have frequently been the target of disinformation campaigns designed to attack domestic levels of trust, often, but not only, originating in Russia. And while Donald Trump shows no hint of regret or embarrassment at benefiting from Russian measures to confuse the American public and undermine the Democratic Party in particular, the truth is that this was never only about helping him. Russia's interest is not partisan but strategic.

The idea of splintering Americans certainly aligned Trump's campaign strategies with Russia's operational strategies. But foreign efforts in disinformation and division were under way well before the 2016 election, and they will persist long after the Trump administration is consigned to history. If we are to protect ourselves, we need to better understand that the strategy is to target trust itself.

In 2018, two years after Russian manipulations to benefit Trump had been exposed, and two years before the concept of vaccines took on a whole new level of importance, a thorough research paper on Russian bot activity appeared in an academic journal. The journal was not a publication on cybersecurity, politics, or international affairs, but the *American Journal of Public Health*. Its authors analyzed more than a million tweets over a three-year period beginning in the summer of 2014. What they found was more subtle but also perhaps more revealing than any of the more blatant election-twisting activity to follow.

The researchers determined that accounts identified as Russian trolls were significantly more likely to post on the subject of vaccination than the typical social media users.

The approach was more complex than to simply blast out anti-vaccination messaging. Rather, the trolls engaged in a kind of malicious "both-sides-ism" that was designed to undermine trust. As the researchers explained:

> *Content from these sources gives equal attention to pro- and antivaccination arguments. This is consistent with a strategy of promoting discord across a range of controversial topics—a known tactic employed by Russian troll accounts.*

By promoting a cloud of "fifty-fifty" messaging on a matter of settled medical and scientific consensus, the overall effect was to create doubt in the truth. The cleverness was in the tactic of elevating people's exposure to anti-vaccine propaganda, all while seeming not to put a thumb on the scale. It undermined vaccine science, while also serving a broader goal of adding to controversy as such. As the study's authors found, "Russian trolls promoted discord. Accounts masquerading as legitimate users create false equivalency, eroding public consensus on vaccination."[14]

As with the troll activity that benefited Trump, there is near-term effect and a deeper strategy. To the extent these messages had the effect of reducing public trust in vaccines, U.S. public health is collateral damage. But it is doubtful that Putin had made it a strategic priority to create more measles outbreaks in America. The bigger goal was to create controversy and doubt. The virtue of going after a topic like vaccinations came precisely from the fact that the issue is settled within institutional medicine, yet still controversial in some corners of the public. Exploiting and widening this gap between people and experts was a way to undercut Americans' sense of trust in institutions themselves, and even in a shared reality. This, in turn, serves to undermine the credibility of the American government among its people, weakening America's strength at home and ability to shape events abroad.

What Russia, led by KGB veteran Vladimir Putin, understands is that trust is a national security asset, critical to the strategic position of the United States, and therefore a high-value target. Troll activity sows division, weakening the trust that any society—but especially a democratic one like our own—needs in order to function well. Adversaries seek out the vulnerabilities in our foundations of trust, just as if they were targeting the weak points in our critical infrastructure or weapons systems.

Of course, for a weakness to be exploited, it must exist in the first place. And in their efforts to sow seeds of distrust in America, foreign actors have had a great deal to work with besides vaccine paranoia. Russia was able to attack American cohesion and democracy using not just fake news but real fissures, many of them involving class resentment, race, and income inequality. At every turn, they have sought to direct their attacks at our most sensitive weaknesses. Is it any wonder, then, that so much of what they do centers on the distrust created by endemic racism?

Indeed, as the Mueller report details, Russian disinformation targeted Black audiences in an attempt to depress turnout for Hillary Clinton. Five days before election day, for example, the Organization of the Main Intelligence Administration, or more familiarly the GRU, promoted an ad on an account it controlled called "Blacktivist," urging African Americans to vote for a third-party candidate, Jill Stein. Meanwhile, parallel efforts worked to target white resentment. According to a University of Oxford report:

> *Messaging to conservative voters sought to do three things: repeat patriotic and anti-immigrant slogans; elicit outrage with posts about liberal appeasement of "others" at the expense of US citizens; and encourage them to vote for Trump. Messaging to this segment of voters focused on divisive, and at times prejudiced and bigoted, statements about minorities, particularly Muslims.*[15]

A Senate investigation later examined the activity of Russian entities like the Internet Research Agency, a state-backed trolling operation. The report found that ninety-six percent of the IRA's activity on YouTube had to do with "racial issues and police brutality," and two-thirds of its Facebook ads were related to race.[16] As Senator Kamala Harris insightfully remarked in her presidential campaign, by exploiting racism and racial divisions, "Russia exposed America's Achilles' heel."

These efforts did not stop after election day 2016. American intelligence officials told the *New York Times* that Russia has continued since 2016 to use social media to exploit racial wounds. An internal Russian document exposed in 2019 even proposed stoking a Black separatist movement in the United States as a way of deepening discord.

The impact of these efforts should not be measured in election tallies alone. It should be measured in the viciousness and even violence they have helped to stoke. And it can be measured in terms of the distortions they deepen within the American psyche, pushing millions of Americans further into the realm of paranoia.

* * *

AFTER A YEAR OF campaigning in Iowa, from coffee shops and backyards in the winter and spring to the famous Polk County Steak Fry in September and the Liberty and Justice Dinner that filled the Wells Fargo Arena in November, the hard work by dozens of organizers and thousands of volunteers had built up to this: February 3, 2020. Iowa Caucus Day.

Like every election day I'd experienced as a candidate, it was intensely nerve-racking, but this one was unlike any time I'd been on the ballot before—not least in that there was no ballot, as such. In the Iowa caucus process, everything takes place in public, as voters literally stand for you on the buffed wooden floors of a high school gym or around folding tables in a community center, gathering in the designated corner of their chosen candidate to be counted in front of their friends, neighbors, and often reporters. This meant there would be no early morning polling site visits to shake hands before dawn as volunteers waved candidate placards while voters lined up; rather, the caucuses began at seven p.m. But the open nature of the caucuses also meant that results could be pieced together swiftly, in real time.

Pacing across the carpet of our suite at the Des Moines Marriott in between clusters of friends, family, staff, and an eclectic range of appetizers that included cheese and olives, pretzel bites and veggie dips, pizza slices and chicken wings, I must have been driving everyone nuts. "Anyone know anything?" I would call aloud every few minutes, to no one in particular. It was more of a joke than a question—of course no one knew anything yet.

I had worked on two speeches, one in case we had a good night, and another in case we didn't. We expected to do well, but there was no way to know for sure. Not wanting to use the word "defeat" even in theory and feeling a bit superstitious, the team suggested calling the latter speech the "Alamo draft." Fidgeting with a foam football a friend had brought into the room to toss around and work off nervous energy, I tried to remember if anyone had made it out of the Alamo alive.

Spent Diet Coke cans accumulated on every surface in the room as we eyed live TV news reports from the most prominent caucus sites. As the results started to come in, it soon became clear that we wouldn't be needing the Alamo draft. In addition to the "anecdata" coming in from the scattered news reporters, our organizers and volunteers were feeding back numbers from caucus sites into a central boiler room, and the results were phenomenal. We were crushing it, especially in the counties that had notably voted for Barack Obama by big margins in 2008, only to swing and support Donald Trump by equally big margins in 2016. It was evidence of one of the central promises of my campaign: that with the right approach and a plan for reaching out to everyone, you could run as a strong progressive and still do well in the more conservative and swing areas—the kinds of places that a Democratic nominee would need to win in November, in order to prevail. And we were also seeing very encouraging numbers in the cities and suburbs. Our strategy had worked.

I tried to contemplate what this moment could mean, to feel the potential meaning of this experience. But by this point I was too tired to do much contemplating, or experience anything besides a numb awareness of everything happening around me. I caught my own eye faintly reflected in a window overlooking the lights of downtown Des Moines, wondering if the man in the white shirt looking back at me was in fact going to be our party's nominee. Then I looked across the room as staff huddled in clusters over laptops, poring over numbers and glancing back up at the TV screens. These team members had upended their lives, as Chasten and I had, to be part of what seemed at first like an unimaginably steep climb. Many had been teased by friends in the political world for attaching their professional reputations and their hopes to this longest of long shots—and now we were on the cusp of winning the first nominating contest of the 2020 presidential election.

I thought back to the hand-me-down metal desks and the fraying carpet in our first campaign office, a three-room suite on the eighth floor of a historic downtown South Bend office tower on the same block as the County-

City Building, its vibe faintly recalling that of a film noir private detective's office. The day I had launched my exploratory committee on the sidelines of the U.S. Conference of Mayors in what now felt like the ancient month of January 2019, our operation had consisted of four staff and about as many interns. One staff member had been hired that same morning, on a handshake, to help organize the press conference where I announced my intentions to about a dozen reporters whose faces looked something between indulgent and quizzical. Now this same campaign had hundreds of staff across the country, had attracted thousands of volunteers and hundreds of thousands of grassroots contributors—and was poised to win the Iowa caucuses.

The big televisions on the wall, muted, kept showing partial numbers, in between clips of me and the other candidates campaigning, as we waited for the official counts to confirm what seemed like a miracle unfolding on my staff's laptops, one precinct at a time. Unheard-of by most Americans just one year earlier, our campaign had out-competed senators, governors, cabinet secretaries, and even a former vice president. And in the process, I would become the first openly gay candidate to win a state in a presidential nominating contest—doing so as the first out elected official even to make the attempt. Our numbers were right where they needed to be, and lined up with the partial data coming from press reports. Now we needed the party to come in with the formal counts and make it official. So we waited, polishing the draft of the speech. And waited, fielding encouraging texts and calls. And waited, beginning to wonder what could be taking so long.

The math around caucuses is complicated, especially because the customary fashion for determining the winner is a formula called "state delegate equivalents," based on the size, turnout, and preferences of each precinct. Our campaign strategy had accounted for this system, but I had always found it confusing, and it made it tough to parse the raw numbers coming in from around the state. What we knew was that we seemed to have an edge in these "SDEs," and I was neck-and-neck with Senator Bernie Sanders in the popular vote.

I didn't yet know whether we could claim a clear first place or a close second, but it was already clear that either case would be an enormous victory. It would mean that our campaign, which almost everyone would not have placed in the top twenty when it began, had risen from obscurity to the top of a large and contentious heap. It would propel us to New Hampshire with new energy and new momentum—as well as a needed wave of fundraising—and if history was any guide, it would position us for a shot at victory there, too. Millions of people take a closer look at the winner of the Iowa caucuses. It is the kind of opportunity no campaign can manufacture. But for any of that to happen, first there had to be official confirmation.

I kept alternating between the couch where Chasten, my mother, and his mom had settled in, and a table nearby where a team member was working on the speech. Even the longest-running caucus sites had now reported, but still, official numbers didn't come in. And no one could fathom the reasons for the delay. Reports started to indicate trouble tabulating the totals or getting anything confirmed by the state party, which administers the caucus. Journalists began reporting that an app that election officials were supposed to use to send in their results was not working properly.

It wasn't clear how to proceed, as a frantic rush into prime airtime began, still with no one knowing what the official results were. The other candidates started giving their speeches, taking advantage of the free live nationwide TV exposure even though the results were unofficial, even those whose unofficial results were unflattering. An airplane—not our usual twin-prop six-seater but a jet with enough seating to accommodate a contingent of traveling reporters—was sitting on the tarmac at the airport, ready and waiting to take us to New Hampshire, but Iowa was supposed to be *over* before we left the state. As it got closer to midnight, it became clear that if I wanted to give a caucus-night speech at all, I had to do it now.

Thrilled with our internal numbers and the fact that one way or another our placement in Iowa had been a spectacular triumph, I stood in front of my supporters to thank them for their work and congratulate them. Shifting my gaze between the words of my speech and the crowd, I kept catching the eyes of Iowans I had met along the way, representing countless people who had rearranged their lives to be part of this effort: a pre-kindergarten teacher who worked part-time at a grocery store to make ends meet and spent her one day off per two weeks volunteering, a precinct captain who had overcome crippling anxiety to become one of our most successful vote-wranglers, and, mixed in with them, friends from every stage of my life who had hit the road to be part of this. It felt good to join them and share the one thing we did know, by any reckoning of the results: "We are going to New Hampshire victorious!" That much was clearly true. But the actual ability to confirm that we had come in first place in the delegate count didn't come that night, or the next day, or the next. And neither, in turn, did the electrifying momentum we were counting on.

This was frustrating enough. But out in the Twitterverse, things got weirder. Social media accounts started suggesting that I was somehow responsible for the reporting delays. An NBC news column summarized the theory:

> *Buttigieg—runs the conspiracy theory—with the help of the Democratic Party Establishment, the developer of the app that was supposed to be used to tally the results of the caucuses and somehow the Iowa Democratic Party (and details on this are fuzzy) manipulated the app (or the entire process) to fail so he could gleefully declare victory and begin his march to New Hampshire with people believing he had won when he hadn't, thereby sucking up more money and media time than he deserved.[17]*

I tried to get my head around how someone could believe this in good faith. And though I know conspiracy theories aren't always held to a high standard of logic, I couldn't get over how perfectly backward it was. Not only had we not caused the delays; ours was the campaign that the delays had most harmed.

Before I got into the race, I had thought I was already

reasonably familiar with various forms of conspiracy theories and paranoid thinking. There was the afternoon of frantic calls to my mayoral office by residents freaked out by a mysterious unmarked airplane repeatedly flying over town, which turned out to be a Navy 757 using our airport for low-approach landing practice. There was the neighbor convinced that the government was widening roads in order to intimidate citizens. There was enough anti-vaccine agitation that I started inviting news crews to come along and broadcast my getting a flu shot, just to try to reassure the public that it was easy and safe. (It may not have had the same public health impact as Elvis getting a televised polio shot in 1956, but I figured it couldn't hurt.)

Still, nothing could have prepared me for the level of conspiracy thinking that comes your way when you become a serious candidate for the presidency. As soon as a campaign starts to look viable, strange allegations begin flying around social media. There was one that said I was a secret CIA asset. Another claimed I'd been arrested for killing no fewer than five dogs as a teenager—complete with a faked, nineties-era *South Bend Tribune* front page. At one point, I was accused of being responsible for a Canadian bread price-fixing scheme that had started in 2002.

Often there was a thin connection tying the conspiracy to actual fact. I was a military intelligence officer, after all, and I did in fact spend several months as a consultant for a Canadian grocery chain that later got into trouble over the bread prices. Conspiracy theories work best, it seems, when the adherents grasp a shred of partial information, leading to more questions than answers. Over time I came to accept this as part of being well known. You could think of it as inevitable math: if a hundred million people know who you are, and one-tenth of one percent are inclined to believe something absolutely bizarre about you, that makes a hundred thousand conspiracists, equivalent in numbers to the whole population of my hometown. And every one of them seemed to have a Twitter account. Those voices would then inevitably be amplified by Russian bots and right-wing media. It was an irritant, to be sure, but I knew it was the inevitable cost of traction and visibility, and it rarely bothered me personally.

But I was admittedly frustrated after Iowa. The conspiracies multiplied. Someone noticed that our campaign had purchased software from the same software company that made the flawed app in Iowa—enough to send the Twittersphere into a tailspin. A staff member on my campaign was married to someone who ran a company that invested in the company that made the app—clear evidence! No one really took the trouble to explain what all these tidbits were supposed to amount to, but then, conspiracy thinking is not obliged to answer questions; it merely asks them, insinuating.

The noise came from different corners of the political landscape in America—and, as expected, from overseas. Some of it came from supporters of rival campaigns; even a Democratic member of Congress retweeted a post that amplified the app conspiracy. On the other side, the Trump campaign gleefully joined in at the chance to divide our party, with people like Trump campaign manager Brad Parscale and Donald Trump Jr. making sure to contribute to the chatter. And later reporting would find, unsurprisingly, that Russia-linked accounts quickly went to work amplifying accounts that claimed something suspicious about the app in Iowa.[18]

It would be easy to dismiss this as so much noise, to assume that something so far-fetched and outrageous would have little impact on public opinion. But a few weeks after Caucus Day, a Pew Research poll found that thirty-two percent of Americans thought there had been intentional efforts to delay the Iowa caucus results, and another twenty-eight percent weren't sure.[19] Remarkably, and with surprisingly little effort, conspiracists had convinced sixty percent of the population that it was at least possible that something had gone maliciously wrong in Iowa.

This is made possible, in part, because social media makes viral amplification so easy. But in a society where there were high levels of trust in media and in political figures, such a theory would be unlikely to get nearly that far. That is not our world today; and when no one's word is authoritative, any crank is as credible as the next person. It is the irony at the heart of conspiracy thinking: you can't trust anyone these days, so you may as well place some credence in some stranger who just tweeted something exciting, if unproven.

This brings up something else about paranoid thinking that is deeply ironic, yet unmistakably present: its appeal to the desire for belonging. We don't usually think about "belonging" and "conspiracy theories" in the same sentence, but I think that our isolated and sometimes lonely age has people looking for connections wherever they can find them. The appeal of paranoia, in this sense, is actually that it simulates the creation of a trusted community. When someone whispers, "Trust no one," they are inevitably also saying, "Trust me," suggesting that you can believe in *them* because they are so skeptical, and therefore credible. To authenticate this, they are doing the favor of giving you that vital secret, the thing everyone else out there "doesn't want you to know." They solicit your trust by entrusting to you an insight about just how untrustworthy everyone else is. Bringing someone into your conspiracy theory, strangely, is a performance around the theme of trust.

For all their celebration of the outsider ethos, fringe groups trade in the alluring opportunity to be an insider of sorts. Many of the most salient conspiracy scenes today, like the Trump-friendly QAnon, have symbols, flags, inside jokes and terminology (like the slogan, "Where we go one we go all"), and ways for adherents to find each other in person or online. In other words, they have all the accoutrements of a kind of *membership*.

Paranoid thinking is hardly unique to our moment. It can be found throughout our recent history—from the bizarre theories about the Clintons to the rhetoric of McCarthyism. John F. Kennedy's opponents accused him of secret allegiance to the pope, while some Americans claimed Franklin Roosevelt had advance knowledge of the attack on Pearl Harbor. Richard Hofstadter, in his landmark 1964 essay "The Paranoid Style in American Politics," showed how none of this was new as of then either, drawing a line from McCarthy's style and language, back to Populist Party leaders in the 1890s concerned about "the secret cabals of the international gold ring," all the way through to late-1700s fascination with the Illuminati.

But today the purveyors of conspiracies have more tools at their disposal than ever, making it possible to disseminate dangerous lies on a massive scale and at unprecedented speed. The Internet, which giddy observers in the 1990s envisioned as the basis for a new era of rationality and fact, has proven vulnerable to the power of rumor in ways that rhyme with the lower-tech history of American paranoia through the centuries. Meanwhile, for the first time, a sitting president gleefully amplifies and encourages this, his own political rise partly built on false "birther" claims against President Obama.

And so today we find ourselves in a kind of multi-direction tug-of-war with fellow Americans, all while edging nearer to a cliff. Across fifty years, through a combination of failed policies, amoral technologies, and concerted, deliberate attacks, foreign and domestic, we have lost access to the basic levels of trust that democracy demands. The democratic process is our only means powerful enough to move us to safer ground, but it, too, relies on trust.

All this is happening at a time when the American system of government—and liberal democracy more generally—has been called into question, as illiberal hard-right politics gain ground in Eastern Europe and a dramatically different model, that of China, is being held up by some around the world as a steadier alternative to the American way. It is a good moment to recognize that there have been other critical junctures in American history when democracy seemed to be threatened by confrontation or competition from other systems. In the early years of the Depression, the economic situation was so bleak that many leaders and academics questioned the efficacy our liberal government and market economy, suggesting that communism, or even the kind of virulent fascism that "made the trains run on time" in Mussolini's Italy, were attractive alternatives. Felix Frankfurter noted in 1930 that "epitaphs for democracy are the fashion of the day,"[20] and in 1934 no less an established figure than the president of the American Political Science Association addressed that body of scholars, claiming, "There is a large element of fascist doctrine and practice that we must appropriate."[21]

Now American democracy has come to another such vulnerable moment, even while the legitimacy of our democratic system depends on our ability to use its tools, and to trust one another to meet in good faith on some kind of shared public square. Our interests may differ, our identities may be diverse, and our values may not always be the same. But we can only negotiate among these interests, identities, and values if we stand on the same field of fact.

CHAPTER THREE

Trust for a Deciding Decade

A S THE GLOBAL DEATH TOLL OF THE CORONA-virus pandemic surpassed a quarter of a million people, in May 2020 a group of presidents and prime ministers from around the world joined together on a video conference to coordinate their efforts to speed the development, manufacture, and distribution of an effective vaccine. It was a little more prosaic than the imagery of history books (or superhero movies) might suggest when you picture an emergency gathering of world leaders. Still, it was important and reassuring to see heads of government from Germany, Britain, Japan, France, Israel, and Turkey each speaking about the urgency of the moment and pledging resources to help.[1] A global crisis called for global cooperation. But one absence was hard to miss: that of the president of the United States. For his part, President Trump was ensconced in his residence at the White House, tweeting false information about a deadly pandemic that he believed he could handle by wishing it away.

That same month, as spring haltingly arrived in the U.S., dozens of states ended their stay-at-home orders and began reactivating their economies, often contradicting guidance from the Centers for Disease Control, which recommended waiting for a two-week decline in cases before beginning the process of reopening. Meanwhile, a series of dangerous conspiracy theories emerged—including one that claimed Bill Gates intended to use a vaccination program to implant microchips in people.[2] A poll taken in May showed that more than a quarter of Americans, including a plurality of Republicans and fully half of those who get their news primarily from Fox, believed the absurd story. (How a microchip was supposed to fit through a syringe was never explained.) By June, a study found that most Americans had heard of the viral internet video entitled *Plandemic*, which presented as fact the idea that the pandemic had been deliberately planned; of those, about a third considered it credible.

The less Americans seemed prepared to acknowledge the views of medical experts and stay at home, the more urgent it became to see a vaccine developed so that the country did not depend only on measures like social distancing and mask-wearing. But then came another alarming poll finding, this time not about Americans' opinions but about their plans: fewer than half of the American population said they were sure they would get a vaccine if one became available.[3]

There are always, as we've already discussed, compelling reasons why it's important to build and maintain trust. But these reasons are elevated at our moment in time, as we face a particular set of challenges—existential challenges—that are difficult to solve, in part, because they require something more from us. This is especially true of the two great global threats before us: pandemic response and climate change. They require sacrifice and transformation, inconvenience and expense, imagination and cooperation—all things of which America has proven itself capable in the past. Such challenges can only be resolved if Americans can trust in their institutions and, just as importantly, if the world can trust in America. This is not some distant concern, as the coronavirus situation laid bare. The twenty-first-century crises we were warned about for years are no longer mounting; they have arrived—and they've put us all in immediate peril.

In some ways, the moment calls to mind the 1930s and early 1940s, when isolationist politicians contended that the Nazi threat was overblown (or even unfairly misunderstood) and that the U.S. had no business getting mixed up in the conflicts that were engulfing other parts of the world. Yet when the Nazi takeover of continental Europe and the attack on Pearl Harbor led inexorably to American involvement in the war, the U.S. acted not only to ensure its own security but for the benefit of democracy around the world, cooperating at home and forging alliances abroad, displaying great trust and growing enormously trusted in return. Our situation calls for no less of a moment of cooperation and American leadership, with the notable difference that the adversaries at hand—like a spreading virus and a changing climate—are not other countries but universal threats.

When Covid-19 first traversed America's borders, Donald Trump famously tried to dismiss it, to convince the country it was nothing to worry about, that soon enough it would all go away. After so many years of concocting alternative realities, he must have assumed the strategy would work yet again. But no amount of bluster or denial could overtake the actual reality of the pandemic. The virus spread out of control. Hospitals ran out of personal protective equipment, or PPE, a term that few had heard before 2020. There were fears that the entire health system would be overrun. Without a lockdown order or even consistent guidance from the White House, governors and mayors, with far fewer resources than the president, were forced to take matters into their own hands.

When, beginning in March of 2020, we first locked down, the American people were strongly in favor of bold measures. Polling in late March found three in four Americans supportive of a national quarantine.[4] But no such national action took place, and the president's daily coronavirus task force briefings became yet another series of confusing and divisive performances by the reality TV president. Still, amid the disarray of messages from Republican leaders and White House officials, one figure soon emerged as the most trusted American official working on the coronavirus pandemic response: Dr. Anthony Fauci. By that May, just thirty-eight percent of Americans said they trusted the president for information on the virus, while nearly two in three trusted the seventy-nine-year-old infectious disease specialist.[5]

Fauci had risen to national prominence during the AIDS crisis of the 1980s. After fifty years in public health, he knew that this kind of trust was not just a matter of goodwill but an essential tool for doing his job. Public health strategies, as Fauci had experienced decades before, depend on a population trusting in experts and authorities, because the outcome of these strategies can depend on the decisions that individuals make, and who they choose to listen to. Whether the "ask" has to do with wearing a condom or wearing a mask, quitting smoking or getting a flu shot, necessary steps to keep a population healthy depend on whether people are prepared to hear, and to comply with, the guidance offered to them. Individual decisions are of course not the only things that shape health outcomes: environmental factors, discrimination, and access to health insurance and health providers all play a role. But to the considerable extent that our health is shaped by the choices we make as individuals, those choices are in turn shaped by our levels of trust.

This is what made it so dangerous when Trump and his political cavalry decided to spend much of the lockdown seeking to build an alternative narrative by attacking the very medical experts in charge. From their perspective, downplaying the dangers became more difficult amid Fauci's fidelity to the truth and to his responsibilities as a public health leader who had served in senior roles since the Republican administration of Ronald Reagan. Precisely because he was so resolutely apolitical and nationally respected, he represented a threat, from within the administration, to the president's agenda. Fauci soon disappeared from regular coronavirus task force press conferences and, for a time, was prevented from giving interviews to reporters. By July 2020, the president had stopped meeting with him altogether. The White House even mounted a clumsy effort to discredit Fauci personally, compelling him to remind Americans of his credibility: "I believe for the most part you can trust respected medical authorities." He added, "I believe I'm one of them, so I think you can trust me."[6]

Meanwhile, the president sowed confusion and doubt that would upend any semblance of public health strategy, and set the United States on course to become the world epicenter of the disease, with a caseload that vastly exceeded that of China, as well as Brazil, India, Russia, and South Africa. Conspiracy theories abounded, which the president amplified, and his approach continued to shift day by day in no particular direction. When it was confirmed that masks were a powerful tool in slowing the spread of the virus, he at first mocked the idea of wearing one. He might half-heartedly support doctors and epidemiologists one day and contradict them the next; he repeated lies and distractions gleaned from the Internet and fake-news sites from the podium, and even overruled local officials, many of them Republicans, by holding an indoor campaign rally in Tulsa. In a national emergency, whether a hurricane or a terrorist attack or a pandemic, it's imperative for all levels of government to be as well aligned as possible. But in this case, mayors protecting the lives of their own residents were often compelled to contradict the president, while some governors managed, in short order, to contradict themselves.

The coronavirus pandemic quickly became a grim and tragic national exhibit on the lethality of distrust and confusion. Within a few months of the first lockdown orders, one in three Americans said it had become harder to tell what was true.[7] And by the summer, the virus spread unabated, as confirmed positive cases climbed to a rate of more than seventy thousand a day by the end of July— leading several countries around the world to ban travelers from inside the United States.

Every pattern that drives distrust—from resentment toward the establishment to the loss of shared reality, from the legacy and reality of structural racism to the general fashion of American paranoia and even Russian interference—played a role in creating one of the coronavirus's most dangerous collective co-morbidities. Across America, like a compromised immune system, distrust itself proved a dangerous preexisting condition.

Successful, early containment in America, as appeared to have been quickly achieved in places like Taiwan and South Korea, would have required a huge degree of cooperation between and among governing authorities and everyday people. The same was true for any hope for a quick, safe reopening, since this depended not only on the availability of testing and contact tracing, but also on widespread cooperation around mask-wearing and social distancing. But none of this happened in most of the United States in those crucial early months.

Other countries fared far better. From Norway to New Zealand, many leaders implemented plans and policies that effectively suppressed the virus. The European Union, at first a major center of the outbreak, then did a far more effective job of containing it, making it possible to return to some semblance of normalcy by summer. It is worth noting that these countries also had far-right parties. These countries also had intense and sometimes polarizing political debates. But no developed country saw the level of systemic failure that consumed the United States through spring and into the summer. The countries that did best were those that acted quickly and with high levels of cooperation. And notably, based on survey data, many of the countries that did this most effectively are also countries that place highly in international rankings of high social trust.[8]

As with other patterns of trust, we can see the American coronavirus experience as two sides of a coin. We can think of this as a reflection of distrust in the media, science, and expertise. But we can also see it as a problem of misplaced trust in a president who cared little for his country's (or, indeed, his supporters') well-being. Many were all too comfortable taking their cue from the president, expecting the virus to "just disappear" or "burn through" (through someone else, presumably) rather than threaten them personally. This kind of trust is especially striking because of how little the president's actions lined up with his own statements. Testing, which he seemed to deride on a national level, was frequently and intensively practiced at the White House. And while his campaign insisted that the indoor summer political rallies it organized would be perfectly safe, that same campaign required supporters to sign waivers of liability and assume their own risk if they actually showed up.[9]

When it comes to conquering this kind of enormous challenge, the inescapable reality is that medicine alone cannot solve it. The development of a vaccine is just the end of the beginning; if too few people actually get a vaccine, then it is not the end of the pandemic. As Anthony Fauci noted in testimony to Congress, if fewer than two-thirds of Americans were to get immunized, the "herd immunity" needed to manage the virus might not come about.[10] Of the distrust and reluctance at the center of our public health crisis, Fauci acknowledged, "It is a reality . . . a lack of trust of authority, a lack of trust in government, and a concern about vaccines in general."[11]

In confronting this pandemic and future ones that could easily occur, it is wise to remember that vaccines and therapeutics—technical solutions—are only part of the story. Inevitably, rebuilding trust in expertise and institutions must be part of the cure.

★ ★ ★

Dealing with climate change has a great deal in common with confronting the coronavirus. To recognize the reality of climate change, and certainly to take any meaningful steps to reduce it, it is necessary for Americans to trust people we don't know, who are working in fields most of us don't understand. It requires that we make substantial, transformational changes and investments to reimagine our economy and our infrastructure, while also adapting our individual behavior and choices. All of this, which can be seen as both inconvenient and costly, is required in order to solve a problem whose fundamental physical cause—the behavior of atmospheric gases—is literally invisible. Like pandemic response, climate action requires that we trust in the science, and muster cooperation and coordination where it has often been scarce:

among different levels of government, across the partisan divide, and throughout the international community.

In some ways, the climate challenge is an even harder one in which to build trust than our public health emergencies. Because of the time scales involved, little of what we must do to solve the problem for the long term would show visible results in the near term. At least with Covid-19 prevention we could see in a matter of weeks when policies had succeeded—and where they had failed. But climate action does not deliver the kind of instant feedback, the treat at the end of the obstacle course, that human beings seek. And there is no vaccine for climate change.

Climate action requires two essential forms of trust-building. The first is to build enough trust in expertise that the consensus among scientists can be accepted as the consensus of the people. The second is to build trust in the idea that the effort and investment needed to solve the problem is worth it—even if it takes years or decades to see the fruits of our labor.

Research tells us that countries with higher levels of social trust are more likely to implement environmental policies, and their citizens are more likely to behave in more environmentally friendly ways.[12] And common sense tells us that public support for bold climate policies will depend on a basic level of trust in climate science and those who share it with the public.

Yet even in 2020, fewer than half of Americans agreed with the statement, "Climate scientists can be trusted a lot to give you full and accurate information on the causes of

climate change."[13] It can be hard enough to trust someone when what they have to say is neutral in its effect on
our everyday lives; but when accepting their warnings is
inconvenient or even costly, we are naturally and preemp-
tively inclined toward disbelief. Inevitably, the decades-
long fight over who to trust on climate change has been as
much about our readiness to receive a difficult message as
it is about the actual credibility of the messengers.

In a sense, those who tell us not to worry about climate
change are like the guy at the North Village Mall who did
me out of my baseball cards back in the early nineties. I
believed him, not because I had assessed his credibility or
weighed the evidence, but for the simple reason that *I really
wanted to.*

The good news is that human beings are capable of
rationality, too. We are all capable of being convinced of
things we'd rather not believe. Indeed, one of the virtues of
strong and trusted institutions is that they can deliver the
truth even when its implications are hard to accept. In some
ways, the original forms of established authority among
human beings—religion, government, parents—have long
served to perform just this function. So have later forms of
authority, from academia to media, to the extent they have
been credible. In the Vietnam era, for example, figures in
the press had enough credibility that they could change
national opinion by reporting truths that were unwelcome
for the public and uncomfortable for those in power. When
Walter Cronkite said on his broadcast in 1968 that we were
"mired in a stalemate" and the war could not be won, the

effect was profound. People listened. They believed him. And within weeks, President Johnson announced he would not seek reelection.

It is the nature of the human condition that we are inclined to deny the truth of things that would be painful to face. As the philosopher Michel de Montaigne observed, "Truth for us nowadays is not what is, but what others can be brought to accept." We do better at confronting hard moral and factual truths when a credible and reassuring voice can help establish their veracity, leaving us less room for denial and pressing us instead into the realm of action. The tougher the message and the less we want to hear it, the more depends on whether we can trust the messenger.

This decade opened with some of the most severe climate change effects yet experienced, finalizing the transition of climate change from its origins as a tentative scientific prediction to its present status as an inescapable emergency. Its reach has extended from the Arctic and Antarctic, to the low-lying islands and coastal areas that attracted the most early concern, to every part of the world. When a series of unprecedented storms hit a desert in the Middle East, little attention was paid. But the region sprouted grasslands, and the grasslands yielded locusts— hundreds of billions of them—which arrived in literally biblical proportions to devastate crops and threaten famine in several African countries in the summer of 2020. And while we don't yet know everything about how Covid-19 and climate change are interacting, we do know that climate impacts on animal populations and habitats may increase the animal-to-human transmission that spreads novel viruses. The Intergovernmental Panel on Climate Change—probably the world's most authoritative collective voice on climate science—offers us some hope, acknowledging that while the window for action is swiftly closing, that window does in fact exist. Still, the data is unambiguous about the need for massive, swift action. According to the IPCC's conclusions, the outlook for the rest of this century depends on our ability to significantly reduce emissions before this decade is over.[14] Otherwise, chain reactions and self-reinforcing effects will become all but unstoppable by the 2030s. This means that in the 2020s—this decisive decade—everything will depend on whether Americans can mount an enormous level of trust in scientific findings, in one another, and in partners around the world, and act.

★ ★ ★

IN OCTOBER 1962, facing the greatest crisis of his presidency, President Kennedy sent former Secretary of State Dean Acheson to Paris to inform French President Charles de Gaulle about the Soviet Union's attempt to place nuclear weapons in Cuba. As the story goes, de Gaulle greeted Acheson with characteristic gruffness: "I understand you have come not to consult me, but to inform me." The comment reflected a disagreement about process, and perhaps about policy, not to mention the general's famous obstinacy. But when Acheson offered to show de Gaulle photographic evidence, the French leader reportedly made clear he needed no such verification, and offered France's support: "Your president's word is enough."[15]

At countless turns since the establishment of the postwar international order, America has sometimes disagreed with its allies and our allies have disagreed with America. But despite any moments of difficulty, these alliances persisted and deepened over decades, based on a deep foundation of trust. For much of the late twentieth century, and much of the twenty-first, our allies have been able to count on our credibility—to trust us implicitly, as de Gaulle trusted Kennedy.

I felt the effects of this trust myself, serving in 2014 as an officer on a densely multinational coalition base in Afghanistan. Working among British, Polish, Italian, Danish, North Macedonian, Australian, Turkish, Afghan, and other personnel, I had a sense that the flag on my shoulder represented a credible, leading power. And everything we did was in the context of an alliance that functioned on the basis of trust. Sometimes that trust had been built relatively recently, within living memory. In fact, many of the countries that relied on each other in this alliance had been on the opposite sides of conflict a generation or two earlier.

Once, on my way to get a cup of coffee at headquarters in central Kabul, I crossed paths with the coalition's deputy commander, a German three-star general who radiated intensity and military bearing. For reasons of practicality—given the sheer number of colonels and senior officers—we were not expected to salute superior officers on the grounds of the headquarters. But you always salute a general. Even at headquarters it was rare for me to run into someone so high-ranking, and I rendered a salute as crisply as I could. Only afterward did I think of the meaning of that little exchange in the context of history. My grandfather had served in the U.S. Army when it was at war with Germany, and here was his grandson, American flag on his shoulder, exchanging salutes with a German general from the very force that that earlier American generation had fought—now a close and trusted ally.

Of course, attitudes toward America have varied widely over time and across regions. As many Americans do, I came to understand that better when traveling abroad as a student, during what then seemed like a historically low point for international trust in the United States: the second term of the George W. Bush administration. One wake-up call came in a taxi in Tunisia, where I had landed, in the summer of 2005, to study Arabic. The spoken form of the language did not come easily to me, especially the North African dialect favored in Tunis, but I was determined to use Arabic as often as I could from the moment I hit the ground. My first sustained conversation was with the cabdriver taking me and my overstuffed backpack into town from the airport. The driver seemed to know that for us to understand each other, he would have to speak simply and clearly. But he also wanted to talk politics. Once I explained that I was American, he raised his eyebrows and asked a one-word question:

"Bush?"

The way he asked the question made clear he was asking if I was a fan. Having spent the previous autumn working on Senator John Kerry's 2004 presidential campaign, it was important for me to detach myself, for him to know that I didn't identify with President Bush or his policies.

"*Laa*," I said. No.

Then he asked what, to him, was the obvious follow-up question:

"Bin Laden?"

"*Laa!*" I answered again.

This, I hadn't seen coming. Where I came from, you were either for Bush or you were for Kerry. But to this Tunisian, it was either Bush or bin Laden. He asked this as casually as if he were asking whether I liked Coke or Pepsi, Yankees or Mets. What's your preference? Tea or coffee? Democratically elected government led by a party you oppose, or a global terrorist network hell-bent on murdering Americans like you? He might have just been teasing, but I definitely didn't have a nuanced enough command of spoken Tunisian Arabic on arrival to figure that out for sure. So I changed the subject to weather.

At twenty-three years old, I had been drawn to Tunis by a summer language course whose tuition fee of 380 dinars amounted to less than a full set of Rosetta Stone CDs. Originally motivated by encounters with translated African literature and later hoping to deepen my understanding of the region after 9/11, I had studied Arabic all through college. But until now I had never actually spent time in a country where it was spoken, nor had I set foot on the African continent. Now was a chance to immerse myself in an Arab city—and with it came a chance to learn about America as well, as one of relatively few Americans in the program, by sensing how I was received.

In those weeks, early in the Bush administration's second term, it was easy to feel how quickly feelings toward our country had shifted. In conversations over meals, coffee, and shisha in the Tunisian souk, my classmates, mostly from European countries that had been friendly with the United States throughout our lifetimes, expressed bewilderment at America's post-9/11 conduct. The Iraq War loomed large, of course, and so did the 2004 election in which American voters validated the Bush presidency, which had come about by something of a coin flip in the previous election of 2000. Much more than before the reelection, the American people now fully owned the unpopular policies of our government.

The Tunisian friends I made seemed less puzzled than the Europeans by these turns in U.S. politics, from what I could tell—but, apart from my experience on arrival in the taxi, I found it was harder to get them talking about politics at all, foreign or domestic. This habit made a lot of sense in a country that had been ruled by the same dictator, Zine el Abedine Ben Ali, since 1987. Photos of the president were everywhere, including a giant portrait in our dormitory. He was smiling, looking benevolent and menacing all at once, with hands clasped and pushed slightly forward in an ambiguous grip that could equally signify either the message, "I am delighted to be entrusted with leading your country," or the sentiment, "I could crush you if I wanted to, like a bug between these hands." Occasionally, after getting to know someone well, I could tease out their views just a little. But conversations about politics with Tunisians always felt furtive and sensitive. I had grown up accustomed to talking about politics as a matter of course, even as a form of small talk; here, the topic was risky enough that raising it at all among outsiders was in itself an expression of considerable trust.

I observed one other unexpected phenomenon during that summer overseas, which continued in the next two years when I was studying in England: a proliferation of Canadian flag patches on the backpacks of Western travelers. In airports, train stations, especially any place where there were a lot of traveling students like me, the red and white Maple Leaf was abundant. I knew that Canadians were well-traveled, curious people, but the sheer number of Canadian flags around seemed far out of proportion to the number of travelers that Canada could realistically have sent out into the world at one time. Either Canadian population growth and wanderlust were surging, or something else was going on.

I soon learned that it was largely young Americans who were doing this—much to the irritation of many actual Canadians—as a way to avoid being on the receiving end of negative attitudes toward the United States. The practice first made its way into unofficial travel advice in the 1970s, when the Vietnam War was sending our country's popularity to then-new lows in many parts of the world. Now, once again, many Americans abroad were concluding that it was best to be viewed as belonging to some place other than United States.

The U.S. has always, even in the nineteenth century, aroused strong and diverging feelings in different parts of the world. And the Bush administration and Iraq War had certainly made the U.S. unpopular by those middle years of the first decade of the new century. But trying to appear something other than a U.S. traveler in a Mediterranean city like Tunis or at an airport in Europe seemed excessive to me, maybe even a little paranoid. No matter how bitterly opposed people were to the policies of our government, it was clear when I spoke with them that they didn't hold it against us as individuals. As one Tunisian said to me about the United States, "I adore the people. But politics is a different matter."

The situation had grown worse by the time I got to Somaliland, in East Africa on the Gulf of Aden, a few years later. It was now the last year of the Bush administration, and global suspicions of the U.S. had reached new depths. I had moved back home to the Midwest, working in the Chicago office of the consulting company McKinsey, and getting a little impatient to go abroad again. So I leapt at the invitation from my friend Nathaniel, then a foreign aid worker in Ethiopia, to take a few days off and join him in exploring a nearby East African state that, according to any map available in the United States, isn't a state at all.

If you haven't heard of Somaliland, that's because the United States, like most countries, does not recognize the breakaway republic, instead considering it part of Somalia. But Somaliland has a somewhat different history than the rest of the country, partly because it was colonized by Britain rather than Italy prior to Somali independence in 1960. The various zones of Somalia were supposed to consolidate after that, but the disaster of the Somali civil war beginning in the 1980s led northern regions like Somaliland and neighboring Puntland to seek and obtain a level of autonomy.

Trust

By 2008, Somaliland, with its three and a half million people, had claimed independence for nearly two decades and established a democratic governance process, though the outside world did not acknowledge the self-declared country. The Somali national government in Mogadishu, barely maintaining control over the capital city itself, was in no position to do much about the secession. For Nathaniel and me, who had both studied international relations, the chance to have a look at a functioning Muslim democracy, trying to carve itself off from a collapsed state, was irresistible.

So one day in July I found myself at an airport gate—not for my usual weekly commute from O'Hare to Toronto or New York, but instead a flight from Djibouti to the Somaliland capital of Hargeisa. As the two of us waited, I elbowed Nat and pointed out an approaching Soviet-era Ilyushin turboprop that looked like it had flown in straight from the sixties, with faded blue and white paint and no name or logo, leaving a trail of black smoke as it descended. I wondered who would trust their lives to an airplane like that, only to learn that this would be our ride.

Stepping aboard and looking around at the number of seats that were missing or collapsed forward cured me of ever complaining about a narrow middle seat on a U.S. airline again. It also reminded me of the trust in air travel established by the tight and well-funded regulatory oversight of the FAA, something taken for granted by American air travelers, whose main concerns on board usually have do to with legroom. It was testimony, again, to the routine levels of implicit trust that make daily life possible in the U.S., as a result of institutions and regulations doing their job.

The plane boarded according to a gender sequence: couples, then women, then men. As the luggage hold filled up, crew members started spreading bags around the floor of the cabin, until the pilot (Russian and red-faced) came back from the cockpit to look around, and concluded that there was too much weight. At his command, some of the bags were chucked out the large open door back onto the tarmac, triggering a dispute with a passenger who noticed his own luggage being ejected. Somehow this argument was settled, and soon we were rolling down the runway and then inching up above the scrubby treetops of the Djiboutian desert, the rhythm of the propellers sounding an awful lot like, "I *think* I can, I *think* I can."

On the ground, a dry and steady breeze gave immediate relief from the sticky heat of Djibouti. We found Somaliland to be more or less as advertised—peaceful and secure, at least by Somali standards. Our hotel manager, also a member of parliament in the unrecognized Somaliland government, talked of aspirations for building trade relationships with Yemen across the Red Sea, exporting wool and fish.

We then visited Hargeisa's main market, finding it vibrant with customers and vendors selling gold, food, and other goods. By far the most common type of vendor was a man with a small table covered in enormous stacks of cash from around the world. I'd seen my share of foreign exchange offices in airports, but this scene was almost biblical: a market square filled with money changers. Somalia's economy is based largely on remittances sent by Somalis in places like Sweden, London, Saudi Arabia, Toronto, and Minnesota, and the money changers play a vital role in taking the wired money and converting it for use at home. (Some of them also operate according to a hawala system, like their counterparts in Afghanistan and Pakistan.)

Peering over a stack of bills, one of the men called out, "Where are you from?" as Nathaniel and I passed by, very visibly the only Westerners in the marketplace or perhaps in this whole part of town. This was precisely the scenario in which they tell you to say that you're Canadian, but we just couldn't do it. "USA," one of us answered.

An unfriendly monologue followed, featuring some choice words about America, Israel, and unwelcome travelers. As our new acquaintance shared his views on religion and foreign policy, heads began to turn from shoppers at nearby tables and stalls. My friend and I were drawing far more attention in the marketplace than we had wanted. We began to realize that a small crowd was starting to form around us. Behind my back, Nat saw one man raise his hand theatrically, as if to strike me on the head, then exchange glances with the others, lift his chin, and finally lower his hand. The whole energy of the place changed in seconds. It was my turn to say something.

Unsure what to do, I threw a conversational Hail Mary, looking at the agitated merchant, raising my eyebrows, and saying as confidently as I could, *"Laakum diinukum wa lii diinii."* Your religion for you, and my religion for me.

It's the final sentence of a sura in the Quran about how

Muslims are supposed to speak to unbelievers. I was no expert in Muslim theology, but I had encountered the passage in college and filed it away in my mind. That last line is interpreted in a number of ways, but somewhere in the course of my studies I'd heard that it could be taken as espousing a more liberal sentiment, a sort of live-and-let-live attitude. I had no idea whether this view was widely shared, or whether anyone around here would care, but I didn't have much to work with.

More than I could have expected, it had an effect—maybe because it invited him to consider this perspective, or maybe just because he was surprised to hear these words from someone who looked like me.

He then paused.

"You speak Arabic?" he asked, in Arabic.

"Yes, some."

"What kind of madrassas are there in America?" He tilted his head, curious and a little incredulous.

I thought about how literal to be. "I mean, we have universities." I said. "That's where I learned to speak."

He persisted just a bit and asked me a few more questions about America—earnest, not rhetorical questions. And the temperature of the interaction slowly cooled. The spectators, though, evidently did not speak Arabic and were not following. At one point, one of them said to him in Somali something that must have been, "Where are these two from?"

He looked at the onlooker, then at the two of us, lifted his chin a little, and pronounced, "*Urubbi*." European.

Then in English he said to me, with a nod and the hint of a smile, "You *Europeans* are always welcome here in Somaliland. Goodbye."

We got the message that he was welcoming us to go away, and obligingly got out of there.

Any number of places in the world have any number of reasons to be skeptical of the West. But here was an example of being more respected, more trusted, and even safer, for having been identified not as American, but European. Each leg of the way home, I looked out the window wondering if this was just the ebb and flow of international and intercultural relations, or a downward slide that would not improve in my lifetime. Could America's damaged reputation be repaired?

Events would soon suggest that the answer was yes. A few months after this trip, the Bush presidency ended and America under President Obama swiftly regained credibility and popularity around the world—not just in Arab or African countries but with longtime allies in Europe. At the end of the Bush administration, less than twenty percent of the populations of Germany, France, the United Kingdom, and Spain expressed confidence in the U.S. president to do the right thing with regard to world affairs. By the end of the Obama administration, confidence in the president reached seventy-five percent in Spain, seventy-nine percent in the UK, eighty-four percent in France, which has historically been hard on American presidents, and eighty-seven percent in Germany.[16] But then, in just a few years under Donald Trump, U.S. popularity plummeted. By the dawn of the 2020s, America was experiencing serious competition—not only for diplomatic power and economic primacy, but for the trust of other nations, in ways we would not have imagined even during the Bush era.

As I've discussed, Russian information operations stealthily target U.S. audiences to reduce our trust in our own institutions. But they also work, often just as determinedly, to reduce the trust that international audiences have in America. Again, efforts surrounding vaccinations and public health are revealing. When the Obama administration was working to help Liberia contain an Ebola outbreak in 2014, the Russian state-owned network RT ran a story amplifying accusations that the outbreak itself was the result of an American bioweapons test. After detailing the conspiracy theory, the TV host editorialized: "It's no wonder that Liberians would be distrustful of the U.S. It's great that the U.S. is buying all of those protective kits right now, but it can't buy back the world's trust."[17]

America's strategic competitors understand that trust is a vital strategic asset in a multipolar world. Some of them also seem to perceive it in zero-sum terms, an understanding that has motivated them to put simultaneous effort both into eroding trust in the U.S., and fortifying trust in their own leadership. The Chinese government may ban Twitter within its borders, but its officials use the platform abroad for advancing suspicion of the United States, as seen in their efforts to promote the conspiracy theory that Covid-19 was introduced to China from America rather than the other way around. Meanwhile, in 2013, China launched its ambitious Belt and Road Initiative, investing huge sums to build infrastructure in other countries in a bid to establish greater levels of trust (and, in turn, outflank the United States in terms of its global political and economic influence). As the Chinese Communist Party's English-language newspaper, the *China Daily*, put it: "The initiative, broadly speaking, aims to deepen strategic mutual trust among the countries . . . and rally international consensus on global and regional issues."[18] (Protesting a little too much, the article also went out of its way to insist the initiative is "by no means a debt trap," which is exactly how many skeptics view it.) Another *China Daily* column editorialized in a headline: "Trust Is the Foundation for Belt and Road Cooperation."[19]

During the Trump presidency, of course, trust in the United States was undercut not only by Beijing and Moscow but from right in Washington. Levels of confidence in the U.S. scraped historic postwar lows as the administration actively and intentionally alienated the world, with actions that have ranged from uncooperative to anti-cooperative. President Trump repeatedly threatened to withdraw from NATO; followed through on his pledge to quit the World Health Organization in the midst of the pandemic; withdrew from long-standing weapons treaties with Russia and a multi-party nuclear deal with Iran; withdrew troops from the Kurdish areas of Syria, leaving important fighting partners in the region exposed and vulnerable to slaughter; scuttled global environmental agreements that the U.S. had originally been crucial in negotiating; and in general rarely missed an opportunity to insult or offend another country.

The administration even sought to elevate unpredictability into a strategy; in his campaign Trump said America "must as a nation be more unpredictable," a rare example of a campaign promise that he actually kept. His defenders have tried to use a kind of strategic unpredictability as a justification for his approach, echoing the "madman theory" of Richard M. Nixon, who believed he could get concessions from the North Vietnamese by getting them to think he was unstable enough to introduce nuclear weapons into the Vietnam War.

The approach hardly worked for Nixon, and does not seem to have created much strategic advantage for America under Trump, either. But, more pressingly, even if this is a strategy, and even if it in theory did yield some kind of short-term advantage in international negotiations, it is exceptionally destructive of trust. The formation of trust has to do with predictable, supportive behavior over time. It's especially important for a nation like the U.S., which has historically been trusted with a major, often *the* major, world leadership role. Sacrificing any sense of obligation to be reliable and consistent means reducing America's posture to that of one more nation out there, scrapping for advantage in a dog-eat-dog world. Ironically for a Republican administration, this style abandons any sense of an exceptional role for this country. It trades the reliability of America (at least, America at its best) for the behavior of a skittish and mistrustful, weak and unstable state. There is no way to know if this kind of unpredictability is really a strategy for Trump or just an excuse to explain away the chaos; but if it is a strategy, it is a strategy that sets U.S. trustworthiness on fire.

Should it be any wonder, then, that not the United States but Canada, with its handsome red-and-white Maple Leaf, now stands as the world's most trusted country, according to at least one global survey?[20] The U.S. no longer rates even among the top twenty-five. So much of America's immediate and long-term future depends on how quickly we can reverse this fall.

At the beginning of the 2020s, it is hard to picture a French president—or any foreign leader—willing to accept without evidence an American claim about a sensitive matter, as de Gaulle did six decades ago. Rebuilding that level of trust in full may take decades, which is all the more reason the work must begin immediately to restore U.S. credibility. But America will also need to seek and generate opportunities to build trust more quickly than is usually possible.

The comforting news is that America does have experience making swift and dramatic gains in global trustworthiness, as it did when it rejected the warnings of the Isolationists and stepped forward both during and after World War Two to help lead militarily, diplomatically, and economically. There will hopefully never again be a global experience of destruction that mirrors the wars of the twentieth century. But in the twenty-first century, the destructive power of threats like climate change and fast-moving disease present global challenges of similar scale. Like any crisis, this amounts also to an opportunity: if the U.S. were to authentically resume the mentality of a responsible and world-leading nation, it would be rewarded with a chance to earn trust with unusual speed.

＊　＊　＊

MORE THAN PERHAPS any other country, America defines itself based on our constitutional system. The Bill of Rights is as essential to what it means to be American as the Japanese language, ethnicity, and imperial history are to what it means to be Japanese. Fundamentally, ours is not an ethnic identity but a civic one. This means that for us, even more than for most other people around the world, a sense of trust is not just strategically important, but existentially meaningful: if the cornerstone of American identity is democracy, the cornerstone of democracy is trust.

Many of the most important debates at our nation's founding were about trust—how much trust could be placed in the hands of the people, and how much the people could trust the government they were inventing and preparing to empower. In a sense, the founding itself was a statement on trust, and the Constitution an attempt to structure the founders' beliefs on how that trust could be distributed.

Thomas Jefferson wrote, "I have no fear that the result of our experiment will be that men may be trusted to govern themselves without a master."[21] Not everyone in that period was so sure. Sizing up the early French Revolution, the British thinker Edmund Burke commented: "The effect of liberty to individuals is that they may do what they please; we ought to see what it will please them to do, before we risk congratulations which may be soon turned into complaints."[22]

And alongside the question of how much the system of government should trust the people came the question of how much the government of the people could be trusted by the people. For John Adams, it was a central issue: "The only Maxim of a free Government ought to be to trust no Man living with Power to endanger the public Liberty."[23]

Indeed, the whole of the Federalist Papers can be read as a debate over who should be trusted with what powers. Trust and distrust were a constant theme, as the founders negotiated around the inescapable fact that trusting anyone or anything (including a government) with an important role inescapably also meant trusting it with power. As Hamilton put it in Federalist No. 23, on the question of whether the federal government should be responsible for common defense, "The moment it is decided in the affirmative, it will follow, that that government ought to be clothed with all the powers requisite to complete execution of its trust." And there was no way to do this without, to some extent at least, accepting what James Madison, in Federalist No. 41, called "the possible abuses which must be incident to every power or trust, of which a beneficial use can be made."

The product of these debates was a Constitution that embodies these tensions, both defining and limiting the level of trust placed in the federal government. The Constitution trusted the people with the power to choose their president, but added an Electoral College—just in case. It gave the people the power to choose their representatives in the House, but it handed the power to appoint U.S. senators to state legislatures.

The level of trust given to the people was radical by the standards of the day, but still very carefully constrained. Also severely constrained, of course, was the circle of who got to count as part of "the people" when it came to citizenship: white, property-owning men, to begin with. But by the efforts and demands of generations of activists and leaders, protesters and marchers, mobilizations and movements, this circle widened with each stage in American history. The Constitution's most elegant quality—its capacity to be amended—made it possible for our republic to grow more democratic and inclusive. And many of the most important and constructive steps in American history—women's suffrage, the abolition of slavery, the legal (though at first not realized) extension of voting rights to Americans of all races, the direct election of U.S. senators—came about by means of hard-won constitutional amendments.

This feature of the Constitution was itself an expression of trust: trust in future generations. The founders were flawed men who were also cognizant of their limitations (much more so than some who would come along later, insisting that laws must only be understood according to the exact attitudes of the men who wrote them). They built into the system a way for it to become bigger than their own biases, trusting their successors with the power to improve upon what they had created. Decades after the founding, Jefferson wrote in a letter to a friend: "Laws and institutions must go hand in hand with the progress of the human mind . . . we might as well require a man to wear still the coat which fitted him when a boy, as civilized society to remain ever under the regimen of their barbarous ancestors."[24]

Today we are newly confronting just how barbarous these ancestors' worldview and actions could be, especially in terms of racism and the slavery it enabled (or, better, slavery and the racism that was used to justify it). Yet these men trusted their successors to place into the Constitution as much wisdom and justice as they themselves lacked. The fruit of that trust is today's republic, still far from perfection, yet dramatically more inclusive and more democratic than the founders could have envisioned.

By historical standards, we are in a drought of constitutional amendments. Other than the rather technical Twenty-Seventh Amendment ratified in 1992 (affecting the compensation of members of Congress), it has been half a century since an amendment was added, lowering the voting age to eighteen in 1971. This is the longest America has gone without a substantive amendment since before the Civil War, and not because there is no more need. Many measures are overdue, including an Equal Rights Amendment to officially bar gender discrimination, a fundamental answer to money and politics that repairs the effects of *Citizens United*, and a replacement of the Electoral College so that the choice of the American people actually becomes president every time. We seem to have lost a level of ambition or imagination that was much more common in virtually every stage of American history but our own. The process for ratifying an amendment is far from easy, but it has been achieved at a pace of roughly once per decade since the Bill of Rights. Given that the creators of the Constitution trusted their descendants—us—with the power to improve it, we could validate that trust by taking this power more seriously.

The generations now living have been tasked to make good on the trust that our system has placed in our hands, both to use and to improve the mechanisms of our republic. But not all of this takes a constitutional amendment. Indeed, the process plays out every election day, one collective decision at a time. The vote, after all, is the ultimate expression of trust in the judgment of the people. If the Constitution places trust in the people in theory, the election is how this happens in practice. The moment of election is an enormous exchange of trust, in which the people are trusted to choose our leaders, and candidates and their supporters trust in the outcome of a process by which they are to be hired or fired. The legitimacy of our entire system depends on the trustworthiness of this process.

In theory, such trust in the system is secured by a mix of transparency and confidentiality, including the concept of the secret ballot. We ensure the accuracy of roll-call congressional votes by insisting that our senators and representatives make their votes public. But when it comes to voting ourselves, the reverse is the case. In most American elections, we have an expectation of confidentiality—and we presume that this makes a person's vote more pure and free of influence: in other words, more trustworthy. But the concept of secret ballots also adds to the need for trust in the system. It means you have to accept that your vote was recorded properly, believe that it was added to the tally, and trust that the same happened to everyone else's.

The legitimacy of an election depends on the people accepting the results. And that, in turn, can depend on the choices the losing candidate makes. It was precisely because the 2000 election was marred by controversy that Al Gore's concession speech was so important. When the Supreme Court ordered the state of Florida to stop counting ballots, Gore chose to focus on supporting the legitimacy of the electoral system, rather than insist on his legitimate objections in this case. "While I strongly disagree with the court's decision, I accept it," he said. "And tonight, for the sake of our unity as a people and the strength of our democracy, I offer my concession." The effect of the 5–4 Supreme Court decision, predictable along ideological lines, was to undercut the trusted status of the court itself. But the effect of Gore's concession was to protect the overall electoral system in one of its most troubled modern moments.

Abraham Lincoln considered it of paramount importance that the 1864 election take place according to schedule, even amid the Civil War, and that its results be honored even though he expected to be defeated. In August of that year, Lincoln asked his cabinet to sign a memorandum in which he committed to work with the new president-elect in the event he lost.[25] (His opponent, George McClellan, was one of his own top generals, whose trustworthiness Lincoln had grossly overestimated.) But Lincoln won reelection, and afterward declared: "We cannot have a free Government without elections, and if the rebellion could force us to forego or postpone a national election, it might fairly claim to have already conquered and ruined us." For him, the fact of the election, not its outcome, settled the question of "whether any Government not too strong for the liberties of the people can be strong enough to maintain its own existence in great emergencies."

Voter turnout in Lincoln's 1864 reelection was over seventy-five percent. In my lifetime, the rate of eligible voters exercising their right to vote has hovered a little over half. For midterm elections, it is considerably lower. This makes it difficult to claim that elections really, fully reflect the will of the American people; and it represents an inevitable consequence of people not trusting that their votes are worthwhile. While claims of "voter fraud" are almost always spurious, the role of money in politics and the naked manipulation of district boundaries, or gerrymandering, undercut the ability of many voters to trust the process.

Meanwhile, many voters who are prepared to bring their voice to the ballot box find that they are prevented from doing so. From Reconstruction to Jim Crow to the present day, efforts to manipulate the electoral process have usually been aimed not at corruptly switching votes that were cast, but rather at preventing people from voting in the first place—particularly Black Americans. What once came in the form of poll taxes and literacy tests now takes the form of intimidation and misinformation, of election officers closing polling locations and limits on early voting, of rejection of mail-in ballots via faulty processes like signature matching, and of purging voters from the rolls. Access to the vote, this founding principle of the American system and a hard-won right for Black voters in particular, is cynically withheld today, without apology and with sinister effect.

Increasingly, some in the GOP have stopped even pretending that these voter suppression efforts are unrelated to partisan advantage. In 2019, when Democratic senators proposed making election day a federal holiday—which would make it easier for workers to be able to vote—Senate Majority Leader Mitch McConnell denounced it as a "power grab," as if all that mattered was which party would come out ahead. In 2020, when Democrats tried to include funding to improve access to the franchise in the age of the pandemic, President Trump was blunt in a Fox News interview, saying it would lead to "levels of voting, that if you'd ever agreed to it, you'd never have a Republican elected in this country again."

One wonders if those who actively prevent more voting have considered how their choices ultimately reflect a deep distrust, not just of voters, but of themselves. To believe that your hopes of election depend on fewer people voting is to have a tragically weak level of trust in the value of your own positions, and your ability to defend them. But this level of introspection may be too much to ask; for those who are engaged in making it harder to vote, as McConnell's comments so bluntly illustrate, this is simply a matter of power.

In the 2018 Georgia governor's race, supporters of Stacey Abrams were subject to widespread voter suppression efforts led by her opponent, then–Secretary of State Brian Kemp, who was not shy about running for office while simultaneously controlling the election process in his capacity as the state's chief election officer. In a single day in 2017, Kemp's office had removed more than half a million voters from the rolls—not because they were necessarily ineligible but because they hadn't voted recently. Over two hundred polling locations were closed over the course of a few years. And tens of thousands of valid voter registration filings were held up because of a minor mismatch in things like initials or name formatting, a phenomenon sometimes called "disenfranchisement by typo." Each of these measures disproportionately affected voters of color. Kemp had failed to deliver a trustworthy process, and upon ending her campaign, Abrams previewed her intentions to prevent another election like this one. She urged supporters to resist the temptation "to turn away from politics because it can be as rigged and rotten as you've always believed" and announced, in the same speech that ended her campaign, the formation of Fair Fight, a nonprofit to combat such voter suppression in future elections and make them more worthy of public trust.

Deep reforms are needed, some of which will be the work of a generation. Moving beyond the Electoral College—the ultimate hedge on the founders' trust of the people—is one step that will show greater trust in voters and, reciprocally, give voters cause for greater trust in how their president is chosen. But we must also take more immediate—and eminently achievable—steps to prevent voter suppression, to facilitate voting both by mail and in person, to establish automatic voter registration, to redraw legislative districts through impartial processes, to counter and diminish the role of money in politics, and other actions to make our representative republic truly representative. A more trustworthy democracy will yield greater participation, a greater fidelity to the needs of Americans, and a positive cycle of political trust.

For better or for worse, there is no Constitutional Convention coming anytime soon to confront the real weaknesses in our democracy. Instead, our circumstances and our system yield opportunities one election at a time. The very means of improving future elections depend on the outcome of present ones. Each election is a chance to further build, or to wreck, the trust on which the American system depends. Issues of democratic structure, process, and procedure have never been as sexy as other issues of the day, but we have arrived at a point where it is as important to know what a candidate will do about voter registration as what they have put forward on, say, health care, or taxes, or any other vital issue. Whether voters prioritize these structural issues will help to decide if the 2020s are to be remembered for what we built or for what was torn down.

CHAPTER FOUR

Rebuilding Trust

S O FAR, IN THESE PAGES, MY AIM HAS BEEN TO illustrate the severity of the crisis of trust in America—and the social and political consequences of allowing trust to remain at such low levels at the very moment when our challenges demand such an intensely high level of trust and cooperation. Based on what we've seen and knowing that patterns of trust and distrust tend to build momentum in either direction, it is tempting to wonder if the decline in trust is irreversible. Yet, despite the many ways in which things have accelerated in the wrong direction, there is also cause for hope. Trust is easily broken, but it can also be built—and, where necessary, rebuilt. And the tools for such rebuilding lie, more often than not, in the hands of the people.

Patterns of trust can be transformed, sometimes amid the darkest of circumstances. When the first thirteen Freedom Riders set out to challenge the harshest strictures of Jim Crow, they were fully cognizant that they were risking their lives, given the brutal punishment that had already met civil rights demonstrators in the South. Their courage forced countless Americans who had been in denial about the nature of this repression to witness what was happening, to believe their own eyes, and recognize that the nation was at a moral turning point. And when the survivors of Harvey Weinstein's repeated acts of sexual abuse and violence came forward with their stories, they knew they were risking a great deal—and had many reasons to believe that their word would not be trusted just because it was true. Weinstein, after all, was an especially powerful producer, and our country, not to mention human civilization, had a long track record of turning on female victims of sexual harassment and rape. It must have taken enormous bravery to come forward, when so often so little trust, both in the last decade and historically, was afforded to women like them.

Survivors have often been greeted with condescension, ostracism, or worse, for attempting to tell their story. But when these women spoke out, the effect was to give others courage to do the same, and then more followed, not only in the case of Weinstein but others, and not only in Hollywood but in countless professional environments overdue for a reckoning, as a simple hashtag—#MeToo—signaled that these experiences were not isolated but widely shared, turning each story into part of a transformative movement.

More and more powerful men were exposed for their misconduct amid the awakening that followed—and with this came a widespread shift in the burdens of trust and credibility. A 2017 Gallup poll taken amid the surfacing allegations found that sixty-nine percent of U.S. adults considered sexual harassment in the workplace a major problem, compared to just fifty percent in the 1990s. In that same period, Americans' opinions shifted dramatically, from fifty-three percent saying people were too sensitive to this kind of harassment in 1998, to nearly sixty percent saying workplaces were not sensitive enough in 2017.[1]

The courage of survivors, who for so long had not been believed but whose accumulating voices now finally brought society to a tipping point, made it possible to break the dominant patterns of trust and mistrust. On the one-year anniversary of the movement's emergence, feminist author Jessica Valenti wrote that "the foundation of how these issues are handled is trust: Who is given the benefit of the doubt. Whose word is considered more believable. Whose experiences and lives are thought most important. Who gets trusted," she concluded, "determines who gets justice."[2]

There remains, of course, an enormous amount of work to be done when it comes to confronting sexual harassment and violence, ensuring that survivors are believed, and seeing our society truly deliver equal social and professional empowerment to women. But the swift changes that this movement made possible illustrate how patterns of trust can shift—sometimes in a matter of months or years—in a healthier direction through actions of truth-telling and courage. And in this case, the changes came about not principally by means of a policy decision or a change in law, but a change in culture, spurred on by the words and actions of courageous women.

Mass movements in our distant and recent past, from abolitionism to workers' rights to the Movement for Black Lives, reflect the power and necessity of redirecting trust toward those who bear necessary and sometimes unwelcome truths. We will also need, more broadly, to develop a readiness to better trust one another while our country advances toward a broader and more inclusive definition of who can belong in the trusted community of Americans participating in a common project.

Part of the reason the American founders were prepared to place such radical trust in the people was that their definition of "people," for the purposes of citizenship and political empowerment, was a very narrow group that included only other white, property-owning men such as themselves. The differences between a Thomas Jefferson and an Alexander Hamilton in things like philosophy, profession, or family background were considerable—but those differences played out in a deeper context of sameness. In other words, with all that they unthinkingly had in common, it was comparatively easy for them to build a sense of belonging. And this, in turn, helped fortify for them the possibility of building trust.

America has been at its best when *widening* that circle of belonging, politically and also socially. That process remains glaringly unfinished, but the history textbooks and political speeches of our country demonstrate the overall pride America takes in a track record of hard-fought advances in this direction, and our hopes for the future rest in the belief that it will continue. Yet as the opportunities for full citizenship have expanded through time to include more and more people, the sense of belonging has also become less automatic, less assured, than it would be among a group that more or less looks and thinks the same. A white, middle-aged businessperson who sincerely believes that he "does not see color," and a Black student who is reminded countless times daily of her racialized existence by a society that sometimes seems to see little else about her, may vote at the same precinct location. But they are barely inhabiting the same social reality. Addressing this question—of how to create or enhance a sense of belonging within as diverse a group as the American electorate or, even more broadly, the American people—is central to our chances of building greater trust in our country.

Belonging is a basic human need. Socially, it carries the power to bind us together and motivate us to depend on one another. People who are assured by a sense of belonging are better able to trust one another implicitly; it furnishes a kind of down payment on the process of trust-building. Whatever sources we have of belonging—kinship, ethnicity, group membership, faith communities—are also inevitably sources of trust. Patterns of belonging based on family ties, religious affiliation, or old-country regional bonds have backed powerful levels of trust that facilitate transactions everywhere from New York's Forty-Seventh Street "Diamond District" to rotating savings and credit associations (or ROSCAs) often formed within African and Asian immigrant communities throughout the United States.

As a resource for building widespread trust, the idea of group belonging also carries an inherent problem: the definition of a group entails insiders and outsiders, those who belong and those who don't. If our group memberships are overlapping and diverse, this can still be consistent with high social trust. I might not have the group-established trust that would come by being a member of your mosque, but if you and I are members of the same soccer league and have built trust that way, then we are also points of overlap for both of those circles of belonging, and potentially of trust. From the profound to the playful, from the chosen to the immutable, my array of overlapping identities—as a Democrat, an Episcopalian, a Navy veteran, a gay man, a Millennial midwesterner, a Notre Dame football fan, a dog owner, a *Star Trek* geek, and so on—add up to a set of ways of being an insider and an outsider in various circles of belonging. I've often found that I can strike up a conversation with veterans, even from a different generation who were involved in a different conflict, more easily than most people I have met before. The dog park near our house invites me to interact with a political science professor at Notre Dame whose politics, I know, are radically different from my own, and in the course of the small talk driven by shared dog ownership, identify other overlaps in our various circles of identity and belonging. The more those circles are shaped differently for each of us, the more these identities can stretch and overlap, often yielding first acquaintance, then goodwill, giving us some way to expand the reach of our sense of belonging and trust.

Inevitably, these affinities and identities also clash with each other. The more consequential a certain identity (say, that of being a Trump supporter compared to that of being a Colts fan), the more it can lead to suspicion of those who do not share it. And with online communities tying us more closely than ever to those more like us, we have begun to sort our politics more reliably according to these affinities—regional, socioeconomic, racial, religious—turning them into a kind of bundle. Circles of belonging that once were overlapping have become increasingly concentric. This can lead to even greater distance between politically defined social groups. As Ezra Klein has explained in his study of polarization and partisanship, *Why We're Polarized*, "The more sorted we are in our differences, the more different we grow in our preferences."[3]

Can we, then, harness group belonging, and tap the trust that comes with it, at a level broad enough to encourage trust at a national level? We might—and this would be the greatest value of a sense of belonging to America itself. By definition, American identity is the one group identity whose dimensions can accommodate all Americans. For that reason alone, American identity should be of interest not only to a certain kind of nationalist, but to anyone concerned about deepening our country's reserves of trust.

Of course, in practice, the definition of who gets to be an American has been limited—not just in the restrictions on political power but culturally. This was the subtext of Sarah Palin's remarks about "these wonderful little pockets of what I call the real America," as if Americans elsewhere were less real. (Interestingly, as analyst Nate Silver pointed out, if "real Americans" comprise white, Christian, non-college-educated residents of the Midwest and South, as the rhetoric of the Trump campaign seemed to imply, then as of 2016 only one in five Americans would qualify as fully "real.")[4] Yet America's highest ideals hold out the promise that the country can be a place of belonging for everyone.

A more inclusive sense of nationhood—what historian Jill Lepore has called a "New Americanism"—holds the promise of making room for every kind of American, while offering a form of belonging that can also be a basis for trust among Americans. If all Americans could feel as conscious of belonging to this shared national identity as Americans generally do when serving or traveling overseas, we would have a powerful source of belonging around which to build greater levels of trust. At its best, this sense of American-ness does not diminish the other identities we carry, but accommodates them, fitting our individual and group aspirations to the common project of strengthening and improving the country to which we belong.

There is reason to be cautious about this way of thinking, especially in a moment when the ugliest forms of nationalism—from telling women of color in Congress to "go home" to proposing a giant wall as a solution to America's problems—have propelled a Trump phenomenon that has delivered neither belonging, except to a fractious few, nor trust. To some, the very idea of a progressive patriotism might sound like a contradiction in terms. But this is not a vision for patriotism as a cudgel, as it has been so often and tragically used, to attack the belonging of others.

There is a different and better sense of fidelity to the American project, and a sense of belonging in the American vision, available in principle to us all. The idea of broad access to a claim on American-ness is rooted in the fact that our country's ideals revolve around civic values, not ethnolinguistic membership, nor a common historical pathway into the shared national present. When activists march to insist that one need not be white in order to be a full and equal American citizen, that American families can include same-sex couples, that a Dreamer who lacks citizenship but knows no other country is as American as anyone else here, they are insisting that America actually live up to the possibility that anyone who upholds our basic values of liberty and democracy would fully and securely belong in this biggest of American groups, the American project itself. Part of what they are fighting for is a group identity broad enough to include all Americans, specific enough to have meaning, and purposeful enough to cultivate trust among all who are part of it.

★ ★ ★

BEFORE MY BRIEF EXPERIENCE with war, the highest compliment I could pay a close friend was to say of him or her that I would trust him or her with my life. To say this about one of my roommates in college or a friend from back home was the best way I could think of to express the feeling of knowing someone to be good and trustworthy at their core.

Of course, the expression was purely hypothetical. I might use it while vouching for someone I was introducing, or in the course of offering a toast at a wedding, but if I had actually tried to picture depending on one of my friends to save my life, the mental image would have seemed comical—perhaps with my dangling cartoon-style from a branch off the edge of a cliff.

My perspective changed at Fort Jackson in South Carolina, the moment our combat training drills started to involve live ammunition. For the first time, I found myself conscious of trusting those around me with my life in an immediate and visceral sense. And as I did so—there in training, and then later during those vehicle runs and the occasional rocket attack in Kabul—it was hard not to be struck by the remarkable fact that these people whom was I learning to trust with my life were not my close friends at all, at least not yet. Half the time, they were people I had just met.

Perhaps the most powerful thing about the experience of *service* is that it creates bonds of trust and respect among people who are radically different from one another. People are placed side by side, without regard to their regional, economic, racial, ideological, or other identities (except, of course, for their American identity), and told to get a job done. And in this context, they learn to trust each other far more quickly and deeply than in most other areas of life.

We often think of this famous bond of trust among service members in terms of the specific (and sometimes romanticized) conditions of wartime. Deployed service members are indeed often under enormous pressure, sometimes facing immediate physical danger, and often far from the comforts of home. The whole range of the human condition is on display, and vividly so, in these circumstances.

But the formation of trust in service is not limited to those cases where someone proves to be supremely trustworthy through battlefield heroics and repeated tests of bravery. Wartime can create many opportunities for people to reveal their character, trustworthy or otherwise. In a firefight, someone can demonstrate unfathomable courage, cementing an understanding of their character that could define them for a lifetime based on one experience. But a remarkable thing about the way trust can emerge in this context is in the way it is so often offered *before* it can be corroborated by experience.

There was a deep form of trust operating in the background when I got into a vehicle with someone to head outside the wire for the thirtieth time. But there was also an extraordinary mutual trust required when I got into the vehicle with a soldier or a colleague for the first time. Often, what stood out to me most was not the experience of trying to get comfortable placing trust in them, but the fact of their implicit trust in me, a reserve lieutenant on his first combat zone tour. The first time I drove and guarded my commander, a career DEA agent with any number of crazy drug busts under his belt, I had to be candid: "Sir, if we get into a situation where *you're* depending on *me* with this M4, we're in trouble." Yet he trusted me from day one, long before I could demonstrate my competence. What motivated a passenger like him, or the Marine gunnery sergeant in his eighteenth year of service with a wife and four boys at home, to trust his safety to my judgment and skill, in the absence of experience or proof?

Part of the answer, of course, was the simple fact of the uniform I wore, the ISAF patch on one shoulder and the words "U.S. Navy" on the name tape, which communicated a shared belonging and professionalism. It meant that we were presumably motivated by certain common values and a commitment to our mission, especially in an all-volunteer military where anyone in uniform was there because they had made a decision. There were also the insignia on my chest, lieutenant's bars and a warfare qualification badge, that signified that I'd been trained and certified ready by the military, meeting some clear and defined standards that spoke to my abilities before they could be confirmed by experience.

But I believe the most operative reason we trusted each other was simpler than that: We simply had to. Trust was required, earned or not, in order to get through our days—not only as a function of danger hovering over everything we did, but just as part of what it took to get our job done. The pressure of circumstance required each of us to make a kind of down payment in trust, no matter how well we knew each other. There was no avoiding the premise of Ernest Hemingway's observation: "The best way to find out if you can trust somebody is to trust them."

Wartime metaphors may be overused, especially in our time, either exaggerating our situations or wearing themselves into cliché. But still, it's not unreasonable to apply the analogy of a military deployment to the current general American condition. Our society faces pressure and danger, as we live through circumstances that require urgent and coordinated actions. Faced with challenges like climate change or pandemics, the entire American people are on a shared front, if not in a proverbial foxhole. In this way, our collective success depends on finding shortcuts to the more sturdy processes for building trust that can happen only slowly, and over a greater period of time than we can afford.

For these reasons, I think that service represents not just a metaphor but a major part of the solution. While military service is not for everyone, some form of service could be. And our country already has the tools to create far more opportunities for civilian service than exist today. Fewer than a quarter of those who seek to serve in the Peace Corps are accepted; for Americorps and the military, the rate is less than one in five. There are far more Americans ready and willing to serve than ever get the chance to do so. As mayor, I swore in Americorps volunteers who would undertake sustainability projects that benefited individual families and our community as a whole; and as a candidate, I met countless Americans who described how their volunteering and service experiences had enriched their lives with skills, purpose, and relationships.

Americans, especially (though not only) young Americans, should be able to experience the formation of trust and connection with very different team members as I did, and without necessarily having to go to Kabul or Baghdad. A voluntary service program, building on existing mechanisms like Americorps, the Peace Corps, and the military, holds the promise of placing millions of diverse Americans in challenging, meaningful situations where they will have to build trust quickly in order to meet their mission. If these positions are decently paid so that service is not a luxury, and if we cultivate a societal expectation that young people in particular should seek an opportunity to serve, we could quickly see civilian service become a national norm.

For the rest of their lives, those who have served would benefit from the experience of forming trusting relationships with people who might not otherwise have crossed into their various circles of identity. It would reinforce an

additional identity—that of belonging to America itself—
among people who might have had nothing in common
the day they met besides belonging to the same national
project. Whatever it takes to deliver this widespread opportunity to serve would amount to a generational investment
in social trust.

★ ★ ★

EVERY YEAR, an influential assembly of global leaders
comes together in Davos, a Swiss alpine town now better known for conferences than snowy peaks, for a multi-
day gathering hosted by the World Economic Forum. In
2019, Dell computer founder and billionaire Michael Dell
was on a panel discussing the theme of inequality, when
he was asked about a newly salient conversation in Washington: the taxation of billionaires like him. Alexandria
Ocasio-Cortez had just arrived in Congress, and along
with a number of prominent progressives, she was calling for significantly higher tax rates on the wealthiest
Americans—to the tune of a seventy percent top marginal
tax rate—in order to fund a transformative policy agenda.
What, the moderator wanted to know, did Michael Dell
think of that?

"No, I'm not supportive of that," replied one of the richest men in the world. "And I don't think it will help grow
the U.S. economy." Asked to elaborate, he continued assur-
edly, "Name a country where that's worked. . . . Ever." As
he paused for what he expected to be a dramatic and con-
firmatory silence, a fellow panelist, the MIT economist

Erik Brynjolfsson, gave the blindingly obvious answer. "The United States."

The murmur in the room suggested that this was a revelation for many of the attendees. Even the panel's moderator stepped in, amid awkward laughter, to suggest that this was only true "briefly . . . in the eighties."

"No, no, no," replied Brynjolfsson. "From about the 1930s through about the 1960s, the [top] tax rate averaged about seventy percent. At times it was up at ninety-five percent. And those were actually pretty good years for growth."

Indeed they were. Between 1948 and 1973, real GDP grew 170 percent in the United States and per capita income nearly doubled. During that same period, the revenue collected through that progressive tax code made it possible to build an interstate highway system and fund the space program, while dramatically expanding the social safety net, with new programs like Medicare, Medicaid, Head Start, and food stamps. Even with historically high tax rates on the wealthiest Americans, the period of economic expansion came to be viewed as a golden age of capitalism. And with government largely delivering for people in a way they had not seen before, these years were also not coincidentally an age that saw Americans two to three times more likely to express trust in their government than they have in more recent years.

This dynamic, in which higher top tax rates and high trust levels are correlated, is visible not only in the recent American past but in the Scandinavian present—a place progressives often look toward, when seeking global examples to emulate.

The Nordic nations have had some of the highest taxes in the world, which are broadly supported because citizens believe they are getting a high level of value for their money. These countries boast low inequality, high education rates, excellent health—and, importantly, a robust private sector. A Swedish baby can expect to live about ten years longer than the global life expectancy, and nearly four years longer than the typical American.[5] The rate of maternal mortality in America is nearly five times higher than it is in Finland.[6] Virtually the entire population of Iceland's three- and four-year-olds are enrolled in early education; in the United States, the figure is just over half.[7] The Nordic countries account for five of the seven highest-ranking countries when it comes to self-reported happiness.[8] And economic mobility—the chance of someone born into a low-income family making it to the middle or upper rungs of the economic ladder—is far more robust in these countries than in the U.S. At one presidential debate I pointed out that based on statistics, the number one place to live out the American dream right now is Denmark.[9]

This Nordic prosperity is relatively recent. The Chicago neighborhood of Andersonville, the Norwegian Independence Day parades in Wisconsin, the roots of Lutheranism in Minnesota, and a rich, century-old Scandinavian-American literature all speak to waves of immigration during tougher times. Much of it was driven by grinding poverty and even food insecurity during the nineteenth and early twentieth centuries. But by the beginning of this century, the Nordic nations had taken their place among the most prosperous countries in the world.

And while circumstances are distinct in each of the Nordic countries, what they now all have in common is a robust social democracy that takes care of its citizens and rewards higher rates of taxation with first-rate services that drive more widespread well-being. So how did they do it? It's one thing to acknowledge the value of social democracy; it's another to get citizens to support the cost of funding it. An enormous part of the answer, it turns out, is trust. Nordic leaders recognize this explicitly. In a 2017 report by the Nordic Council of Ministers, entitled *Trust: The Nordic Gold*, the authors conclude that it is "difficult to imagine societal models like those in the Nordic countries if citizens do not trust that other citizens also contribute to the economy through the tax system, and that public authorities manage tax revenues in a fair and efficient way, free from corruption." Put another way, higher taxes are possible because of high levels of trust, and high levels of trust are possible because the system is considered fair.

America, of course, is not Scandinavia. Countless cultural and institutional differences shape politics and society here very differently than in the Nordic states—most notably our country's past history and current patterns of racial discrimination. But we can learn important lessons here, not just about how well-funded institutions can deliver for citizens, but about how robust levels of public investment are connected to levels of trust. And we can see how these investments in better schools, child care, transportation, health care, and so on have yielded positive results—in turn strengthening trust and willingness to support such investments, in a positive and self-reinforcing cycle.

Here in the United States, a comparable cycle is at work, but in the opposite direction. The levels of income inequality we now experience in America amount to a glaring policy failure. The explosion in inequality over the last half century has not been an inescapable consequence of capitalism but the result of a series of policy choices, many of them tax-related. As Americans observe companies like Amazon, in some years, paying zero in taxes on billions in profits, confidence in the basic fairness of the tax system has eroded. Even Warren Buffett has expressed bewilderment at the fact that his own secretary is effectively taxed at a higher rate than he is.

The slashing of taxes, and the opening of loopholes, have had a clear and direct cost: degraded services and yawning deficits that give the entire mission of government a bad name. As road and water infrastructure fail, as digital infrastructure in rural parts of the country remains nonexistent, as underfunded education systems continue to fall behind international peers—all in ways that hit hardest for Americans of color—the overall effect is to diminish trust in our collective capacity to solve problems. And so it becomes routine for Americans to express offhanded dismissal about the capability of government to do anything at all (hence the fashion for commenting on some failure by huffing sarcastically, "Your tax dollars at work").

And so, perversely, it becomes easier for politicians to argue *against* the levels of taxation we would need in order to fund a more effective government and reduce income inequality (or, indeed, even to sustainably fund the safety net we have today, which is affordable in principle but not within our current tax structure). Resources dwindle, deficits widen, services degrade further, to the point that the U.S. has slipped by many measures into the lower ranks of the developed nations. The Covid-19 experience, in which Americans for the first time in our lives witnessed most other countries rejecting American travelers in order to protect their own populations' health, has lent a humiliating and dramatic illustration to a broader slide in standards of development, which has been under way now for decades. Amid poor results, trust erodes. And the cycle continues. The very same circular pattern of trust, taxation, delivery, and further trust that works so well for Scandinavia is working in the opposite direction in America. The question, of course, is how to break that cycle.

Cycles, virtuous and vicious, are familiar to any mayor. So many of the phenomena that cities deal with—the popularity of a business sector, the reputation of a school district, the working relationship between units of government—are best described as a "chicken-and-egg" phenomenon. And when you are trying to change a dynamic that feeds on itself, you have to find a point at which to intervene. For America, in this equation of trust, our most actionable opportunity is to start by intervening with a fairer tax code. Subjecting top incomes to fairer tax rates, closing the loopholes and incentives that have billionaires paying lower effective rates than schoolteachers, requiring corporate actors to pay their fair share, and further reforms, can both raise the revenue needed to better confront inequalities of income and opportunity and establish a more level playing field for those seeking their own version of the American dream.

Americans will not suddenly begin to trust government if they don't see better results; and government won't suddenly deliver a dramatically higher standard of living if it remains starved of resources, no matter how many efficiencies we find at the margins. It will always be worthwhile to root out waste and inefficiency in government, but the simple math is that this will not compensate for chronic underinvestment or savage cuts. Only if we can muster the political will to tax more fairly and invest boldly in better infrastructure, health, equity, and education, will we have a chance to reset the cycle.

A fair tax system promotes trust. Higher trust in the value we get for our tax dollar means Americans will be more willing to pay for results. Adequate tax revenue makes greater government investments in transformative ideas more viable. And public investments, if managed well, create new opportunities for the American people that, in turn, promote trust—a virtuous cycle with accelerating momentum.

There is of course more to successful government than spending, and there is more to Americans' willingness to part with tax dollars than their reported level of trust in government. But there is little question that a fair and well-funded system will beget a fairer and better-funded system. So if we want the resources at our disposal to rebuild our infrastructure, to deliver health care for all Americans, to combat climate change, and to improve quality of life, we must recognize that a more reasonable approach to taxation in our country is also a pathway for greater trust among ourselves.

★ ★ ★

"WE HAVE LISTENED to the wisdom of an old Russian maxim," said Ronald Reagan, as Soviet Premier Mikhail Gorbachev stood next to him at a White House ceremony celebrating the signing of the Intermediate-Range Nuclear Forces Treaty in December 1987. "Trust, but verify."

Gorbachev, laughing with the president, said to him, "You repeat that at every meeting."

"I like it," Reagan affably replied.

It was an unusually warm moment in U.S.-Soviet relations, but when it came to the expression, it's hard to say exactly what the president meant. After all, the saying, which rhymes in the original Russian, is probably better thought of as a joke than a maxim. The very nature of trust is to accept what someone has to say when you will not or cannot check to see for yourself. To trust is not to verify. To verify is, emphatically, not to trust.

Indeed, one of the things that makes trust so helpful is that verification can be so complicated and expensive. Verification reflects an absence of real trust; but repeated over time, verification can lead to such trust, by establishing consistency. To check on someone is not to trust them. But to check on someone repeatedly and find them reliable is to develop a reason to trust them next time.

New technologies for transparency mean that verification isn't quite as expensive as it used to be. A reporter who used to have to spend hours in an archival basement somewhere looking for meeting minutes from a government contracting meeting can now just find them online. A parts supplier can communicate output and quality control data to its customer in real time.

Transparency makes it easier to verify, and at the same time can reduce the sense of a need to do so. When an institution demonstrates transparency it is also signaling that it is not corrupt. If trust says, "I don't need to check on what X is doing, because I trust them," logic says, "I don't need to check on what X is doing, because they have made it very easy to check, and if they were doing something wrong, they wouldn't have."

This was a very important principle for my administration in South Bend. We already worked within a strong state law mandating the production of records of all kinds, from purchase orders all the way down to emails, and we prided ourselves on being responsive. We even had a party, complete with a cake, in the city's law department when our administration hit the milestone of processing ten thousand requests for city records without a single violation.

I also signed an Open Data policy to push information online in an easy-to-access way—not just the kind of documents covered by open-records laws, but huge sets of data on everything from how our code enforcement department was addressing vacant houses, to line-level information on city spending so people could see how tax dollars were being put to use.

I'm not sure how many people actually looked these things up. But the important thing was that they could. To put it out there was a statement, a gesture of confidence that people who did look in our books would like what they found. (And if they found something problematic, it would be something I'd want to know, too.) I believe this kind of transparency helped to build support for our initiatives, and helped me win reelection. But the most powerful evidence of the relationship of transparency to trust is what happens in its absence. I experienced that firsthand, as well.

In 2012, only a few months after I took office, my administration came into custody of tape recordings that were believed by some to contain evidence of police officers making racist remarks in phone conversations. But because of problems with the legality of how the recordings were made, I was warned that their existence, as well as any action to release their contents, could represent a felony violation of the federal Wiretap Act.

As rumors about the recordings swirled throughout various circles of the city, especially the Black community, and pressure to release the tapes grew, my attention was dominated by the legal risk associated with the recordings—I followed advice not to disclose, or even myself to learn, their contents, without a court order clearing the way to do so. Navigating the unexpected scandal during my first few months in office, I grew frustrated and defensive. The community was, understandably, focused on the substance of the recordings, and I seemed incapable of convincing many residents that I lacked the option they wanted me to exercise.

With the benefit of hindsight, I can see now that the

most important problem was not one of law, but one of trust. Residents already felt they had reason to be skeptical of police in general, were already fearful for their own safety, and every time this story came up, it reminded them that information was being withheld. The more I insisted that it was the law, not my intentions, that stood in the way, the worse it became—because this was a reminder that the very system that had caused so much harm and inequity was now an obstacle to the community's needs. I was operating within that system, and subject to its sanctions, which is why my focus was on complying with the law. But cruelly, it was the law—which is supposed to establish and organize trust in our society—that stood in the way of the transparency that our community needed in order to fully confront a major source of mistrust and pain.

Stuck when it came to the tapes, which became a subject of years-long litigation that continues to this day, I pushed for other forms of transparency around policing—including the creation of a website to help residents track crime rates, the use of force, and complaints against police. And in 2018, I announced the introduction of body cameras to the department.

The cameras could offer both of the benefits of transparency for trust-building: They could make it possible to verify what officers were doing, and they could signal that the department had nothing to hide. It was the most direct way we could think of to ensure good conduct by officers on duty. And, I pointed out to reluctant officers, it also protected them in the event of a dispute when an officer did the right thing. But all of this only works if the camera is rolling.

It was the early morning of Sunday, June 16, 2019, when officers received a call concerning vehicle break-ins at the parking lot of an apartment building in downtown South Bend. Minutes after they arrived, a white police officer shot Eric Logan, a fifty-three-year-old Black father, son, and resident of our city. Traveling that day, I woke in a hotel room to a phone call from my staff with the news, and immediately felt sick. Every few minutes came another call, with worse news: first that he was in critical condition, then that he had passed away. I rushed home to South Bend, knowing that his family, and the community, would want answers. So did I.

That night, in my office, I met with his stunned and grieving family. I recognized one of his brothers, who had come to me the previous year with concerns about conditions in public housing, and whom I had seen from time to time since. I shared the basic information we had, which wasn't nearly enough, and asked the police chief to remain in contact with them and get them as much information as possible as it emerged. Their anguish would soon turn to anger, especially when it became clear that, infuriatingly, the body camera of the officer had not been activated during the encounter.

The whole community was left to wonder not only what would have been shown on the camera, but why the camera had been off. No one had a good explanation, and I was livid, as were residents across the city. For many Black residents especially, this fact matched their worst expectations around policing. A police officer is supposed to represent safety; when an officer kills a resident, it strikes at the core of the relationship between a community and the police officers who are trusted with arrest powers, and weapons, in order to do their job. Now the issue of the camera created another cruel blow to the possibility of trust.

In the days that followed, the pain of the community poured out. I wanted to comfort Eric Logan's family, especially his mother, but whenever I looked into her eyes I knew I was doing so as the steward of an institution that had killed her son, one that was now was unable to provide the answers that she and her family were seeking. I requested an outside investigation, which came back with a determination that the officer's actions had been "justified." But the special prosecutor's findings came in the absence of what we most needed to see: footage of what had actually happened. The officer resigned, but he faced no charges over the incident. And the pain grew deeper.

I knew that part of my job was to acknowledge this pain, to answer for what our city was doing to try to build trust and heal wounds that went beyond this tragedy, to a deeper sense of danger felt by Black residents that had built up through the entire history of our city and country. And I knew that we had to find ways to do more to address it. My office organized community sessions, not only to discuss what had happened but as a space for residents to develop a set of recommended changes in everything from training and recruiting to procedures for discipline. The work continued as long as I was in office and beyond, with the administration seeking to earn reciprocal trust from community members by placing trust in them to propose changes and improvements to how police operate. It will not lead to something as simple as a happy ending, but it created a way for residents and officials to look each other in the eye and work through what it would actually take for everyone living in the city to feel a sense not of danger but of safety when they see an officer approaching. Within a year, every city in America would be moving these questions to the top of its agenda, if they hadn't already been there.

★　★　★

IF HUMANS WERE unfailingly reliable, the concept of trust would fall away, meaningless and unneeded. We would know, automatically, what to expect from one another. It is precisely because we are flawed, biased, sure to make mistakes and let others down, that we grapple with trusting one another. Yet we do manage to trust people and institutions even knowing that they are flawed by nature. Even more remarkably—and importantly, in this moment—we have a profound capacity to restore trust where it has been damaged.

Public or private, our processes of remedy—whether in response to police misconduct, general corruption, ordinary crime, or personal betrayal—serve in part as a means for rebuilding trust in the context of human failure or wrongdoing. In fact, the entire legal system could be viewed as a way of establishing, shoring up, and, where necessary, restoring trust. Contracts are a way of substituting for trust—codifying everything about an arrangement between people or entities that can't responsibly be done with a handshake. They play the role of trust by defining mutual expectations, and by specifically contemplating what should happen if any of those expectations are violated. It is precisely by attention to the possibilities of mischief or misunderstanding that contracts do, artificially, the job that trust could do naturally. And they only work because they exist in a system of law where they can be enforced if broken.

The broader social contract that stands behind criminal law is supposed to play a similar role, not between two parties but between individuals and society. In theory, criminal justice establishes a collective response to breaches of trust between people and the community. In practice, these responses have usually been a form of retribution. But recent years have seen accelerating interest in the concept of restorative justice, which reflects the possibility that criminal justice processes could focus more on reestablishing trust in individuals who have harmed society by harming others. And by demonstrating a broader level of good faith on the part of a system that has often been anything but just, a greater attention to restorative justice could also help build general trust in the criminal legal system itself.

Not only is restorative justice a promising direction in the criminal legal system, it has also proved a powerful principle for collective reckoning. In dozens of countries, a national process of truth-telling has helped to name and confront the wrongs that deepen mistrust at a national level. The time has arrived for us to consider this as a strategy for building trust in our own country.

Perhaps the best-known example of this was the Truth and Reconciliation Commission, established in South Africa as part of the dismantling of the apartheid regime. In exchange for amnesty, individuals involved in abuses offered testimony about their role, while others provided testimony about how they were victimized. The truth-telling was possible because the witnesses had great incentive to be honest. It was credible because these were still painful and inconvenient truths to share. And it was multifaceted, as all sides were there to provide information. What resulted was a shared basis of fact, which would help the country's institutions and its citizens reckon with its history. And it gave victims the power of being heard and believed, their experiences acknowledged in a society that had long treated them with distrust and contempt. By creating a process that established, in hard-to-escape fashion, what the truth really was, it responded to Hannah Arendt's insight that on their own, "factual truths are never compellingly true." Telling the truth before had not meant that survivors could expect to be believed. But the right environment could ensure that they could no longer be dismissed. As Arendt said, "facts need testimony to be remembered and trustworthy witnesses to be established in order to find a secure dwelling place in the domain of human affairs."[10]

A different but related model appeared in the aftermath of genocide in Rwanda, where a National Unity and Reconciliation Commission was established in 1999 and

became a permanent body. This commission did not operate with the same amnesty structure as in South Africa,
instead working alongside trials and sentencing adminis-
tered by a localized system called Gacaca courts and by the
International Criminal Tribunal for Rwanda. Nearer to the
U.S., Canada adopted a truth and reconciliation model as
part of its reckoning with a history of abuse toward indige-
nous peoples that took place in its Indian residential school
system. The system had demonstrated tremendous cruelty,
while also serving to demolish native culture and family
structures. The Truth and Reconciliation Commission of
Canada enacted a national confrontation with what had
happened, and established the credibility of survivors. As
the chair of the commission said, "As [Canadians] listened
to the survivors they were compelled to believe them, and
belief is part of the truth-telling process."[11]

The approach has had its critics. More than twenty
years later, grievous racial inequalities persist in South
Africa, raising the question of what might have been, if
the national reconciliation process had been accompanied
by a more robust program of material restitution or repa-
ration. The Canadian model was part of a settlement that
included cash payments to survivors, but has sometimes
been faulted for "historicizing" problems of colonialism
that did not end when the residential school system was
abolished. And twenty years of work have not been enough
for the ongoing Rwandan process to be considered complete when measured against the enormity and complexity
of what happened there. But many of these critiques might
be taken less as an indication that this kind of process is

not worthwhile, and more as evidence that their truth-telling work is necessary but not sufficient. This, too, is a lesson we might apply closer to home.

The United States hesitates to accept the usefulness of examples from abroad, even from the world's most stable and prosperous countries, let alone those dealing with the aftermath of genocide or apartheid. But we have reached a stage in which America has little to gain from denying that we, too, are a war-torn country with commensurately deep wounds still open. How else can we make sense of the fact that the removal of Confederate symbols was a controversial subject in 2020? How else will we confront the inarguably genocidal treatment of American Indians in our past? And how else can we make good on our nation's moral self-image, unless we can confront the relationship between past wrongs and present ones, manifest to this day in the disparate outcomes for Americans of color?

Done right, this could be an exercise in redemption, not simply a show of guilt. The urge for such reckoning is not anti-American but deeply American, and also highly pragmatic for a country that will not escape its past by hoping it will fade away on its own. "The past is never dead," William Faulkner told us. "It isn't even past." Until we face the relationships between past and present wrongs, and how we are implicated in both, no one will be free. We will hesitate to trust each other, and struggle to trust ourselves.

Fifty years ago, John W. Gardner sized up what he already perceived to be a crisis of confidence in America. He concluded that American institutions were "caught in a savage crossfire between uncritical lovers and unloving critics." Today, the metaphor of lovers may be more useful than that of crossfire; in the same way that coming to love another human being means coming to know them fully, our relationship to our own country requires that we assess her virtues and faults with enormous honesty. Doing so holds the promise of making us more sure-footed, more at peace with ourselves, and ultimately more trusting and trustworthy.

A truth and reconciliation commission has its limitations. But it might very well be the best way for America to fully confront its past so that we can better navigate our present. California Congresswoman Barbara Lee has proposed a Racial Healing and Truth Commission to examine America's racial truth, from slavery to present-day systemic racism, understanding that the past and present are part of the same reality.

Some have even proposed some version of such a truth-telling process as a nonpartisan way to respond to the moral abuses during the Trump presidency. It might be especially useful for a post-Trump Republican Party, by establishing through a process of honest reckoning that one need not be a Democrat to view the venality and corruption of Trumpism as dangerously wrong. As one proponent has argued, "The truth would set the Republican Party free."[12] Who knows what liberating truths it might be possible for Democrats, too, to offer and contend with in this kind of process?

In this sense, some kind of national truth-telling process could offer the basis for a kind of shared moral understanding; a moral parallel to the shared base of scientific fact that our country will need in order to fully understand the decisions that confront us around health, climate, and every other issue.

★ ★ ★

THE FIRST NEWS EVENT I can remember was the space shuttle *Challenger* exploding after launch in 1986, killing the seven astronauts on board, including a schoolteacher, Christa McAuliffe. At four, I more or less understood what had happened, but not the context. Our country had never lost an astronaut in flight across six moon landings and nearly two dozen shuttle missions, and because McAuliffe was on board, millions of schoolchildren watched the disaster live in their classrooms. Most significantly, I didn't grasp what a later investigation would reveal: that NASA had launched the shuttle under unacceptably risky weather conditions. The tragedy was preventable.

President Ronald Reagan wrote in his diary, "There is no way to describe our shock and horror."[13] That night, with the help of his speechwriters, he tried. He had planned to give his State of the Union address that evening, but instead addressed the nation about the tragedy from his Oval Office desk. Nothing is less welcome for a national leader than delivering bad news; but in doing so, Reagan actually cemented his role, in a memorable and poetic remembrance of the astronauts.

One might have expected a failure of this magnitude to have undermined trust in the space program, in the country, and in the president. But soon after his speech, polls recorded the highest job approval rating of Reagan's entire presidency. The disaster was a source of anguish and humiliation for the country, but by acknowledging the failure directly, Reagan demonstrated a measure of transparency that was ultimately reassuring. Embodying our national vulnerability, he generated a level of national goodwill.

Too often, we think of trust as the product of infallible consistency. But trust is just as often about how we handle failure, and in the wake of failure people can be astonishingly forgiving. A year after the *Challenger* disaster, Reagan would address the nation concerning the Iran-Contra affair, which led to the indictment of several high-ranking administration officials. (The spectacle of Lieutenant Colonel Oliver North misleading Congress would deal a blow to the credibility of the uniform of an order not seen since Vietnam.) Many doubt to this day that America got a full and honest account of the president's knowledge and involvement in the plot to trade arms for hostages. But even here, Reagan seemed to benefit from the limited extent to which he did step forward and own what had happened. Little about this episode was to his credit, but he earned a measure of appreciation and even forgiveness from Americans not because of the occasional, fuzzy denials but because he finally said he was "the one who must answer to the American people for this behavior."

Presidents after the Trump era will need to return to the basics when it comes to trust and credibility. By 2020, each of the most important means available to the White House for building trust—transparency, responsibility, vulnerability, truth-telling, predictability, reciprocity—had been not just abandoned but torched. Trump sought neither the trustworthiness that comes from consistently telling the truth, nor the credibility that comes from admitting mistakes. Asked about the removal, on his watch, of the pandemic preparedness unit of the National Security Council, Trump uttered the words that might best sum up his presidency: "No, I don't take responsibility at all."

*　　*　　*

VULNERABILITY IS NOT just a means of earning trust; it is at the core of what it means to trust someone in the first place. If anything is at stake in a scenario where you trust someone, then you are entering a vulnerable state by offering up your trust. Trust itself is sometimes defined as a choice to be vulnerable in the context of others' uncertain credibility. And like trust itself, showing vulnerability is often a reciprocal act.

Every queer person who has come out to at least one other person has felt this. To confide in another about one's sexuality or gender identity is to place oneself in a position of deep vulnerability. Often as I campaigned for president, people would share in whispers or passed notes that they were LGBTQ+, and I was always struck by their trust in me. Sometimes, they were putting themselves at risk by sharing this at all, or in some cases even by being seen at one of our events. Shaking hands along a rope line after one appearance, Chasten and I met a couple who said they had driven eight hours to be there, only feeling comfortable to attend because it was so far from home; they had feared that being seen together at an event with our campaign would be enough to out them in their conservative, rural community. It was humbling to think about the vulnerability people showed at one campaign stop after the other. But then, they were returning the trust I had placed in them by campaigning as my real self.

My decision to come out in South Bend during the 2015 general election campaign was an act of trust and a decision to be vulnerable. While our city had passed an ordinance in my first term prohibiting employment discrimination based on sexual orientation, it didn't really apply to the job of mayor. In our usually Democratic but socially conservative city in the north of what was then Mike Pence's Indiana, I had to ask myself, would I get fired for this? I had to take a leap of trust, that voters would evaluate me based on my job performance—and, more deeply, that they would accept me for who I am. As I wrote in the essay in the *South Bend Tribune* in which I came out:

> *Putting something this personal on the pages of a newspaper does not come easy. We Midwesterners are instinctively private to begin with, and I'm not used to viewing this as anyone else's business.*
>
> *But it's clear to me that at a moment like this, being more open about it could do some good. For a local student struggling with her sexuality, it might be helpful for an openly gay mayor to send the message that her community will always have a place for her. And for a conservative resident from a different generation, whose unease with social change is partly rooted in the impression that he doesn't know anyone gay, perhaps*

a familiar face can be a reminder that we're all in this together as a community.

There was no way to be certain what would come of this. A mayor coming out might have been a non-event in some American cities, but things were different in Indiana. Yet to my relief, the community responded in kind, continuing to trust me to serve them as mayor by sending me to a second term with a higher vote margin than the first time I'd run.

Of course, this is not how it played out for every voter, here at home, or later, when I ran for president. Soon after the Iowa caucuses, reporters started asking me about a video that started making the rounds of the Internet, of a woman who showed up planning to caucus for me, only to change her mind after hearing that I was married to a man. (The fact that this was a surprise to her was its own lesson about how information reaches voters.) It was hard not to think of this situation in terms of trust: How was it that she walked into that caucus location prepared to trust me with the presidency, and all that meant for the well-being of her family, only to withdraw that trust once she knew a little more about mine?

I would still hope to earn her vote if I run for office again, just as I would have aimed to serve her well as president whether she voted for me or not. But I know that the best chance I have of earning anyone's trust begins with honesty. It may be impossible to know with certainty how any number of people will react to anything we reveal about ourselves. But I'm certain that trust cannot be built between people if we do not arrive in these encounters as our true selves.

* * *

TRUST ISN'T ABOUT perfection. It's not about certainty. Trust only arises, is only needed, because we are so often less-than-credible beings. Trust in institutions is important precisely because we can't all be checking on them all the time. Trust in one another matters because we do not have the energy or the tools to be constantly verifying what others will do. The extraordinary power of trust is that it lets us proceed as though we are certain of what to expect from others, when the truth is that we are not.

The truth is that our election system is flawed. But it will only be improved if we trust it enough to *use* it to elect people committed to fixing it. The truth is that our government's credibility has eroded—partly through sabotage but also through self-sabotage—and it will only be improved if we invest in it. The truth is that our relationships are frayed in this country, and they will only improve if we engage in shared efforts, from activism to service to truth-telling, and trust in the power of this work to change our laws and our culture. The truth is that the world trusts our country less now than at any time in memory, owing to failures of both competence and integrity by our leadership. But in this frightening era of climate change and global pandemics, necessity binds people across the world as never before.

Era-defining challenges bear down on us in this season, and we have run out of time simply to expect things will improve on their own. If we can harness what remains in our dwindling reserves of trust; if we can use it to reverse the cycle of suspicion and disappointment that has brought us to this point; if we can build credibility through transparency and deal with the darker sides of our own story—then I believe we can overcome even the most ferociously daunting challenges of the twenty-first century. History and circumstance have placed us at this moment of reckoning. I trust that we can meet that moment, if only because we must.

Acknowledgments

This is not an election book, but I believed that it was important to share these thoughts ahead of the November 2020 elections. As a consequence, *Trust* had to be prepared in a matter of months, which simply would not have been possible without a great deal of support and insight from others.

Inspiration to investigate this subject came from conversations with Professor Meghan Sullivan, director of the Notre Dame Institute for Advanced Study, where the issue of trust has been the focus of a year's work among its invited scholars. I have been honored to join this community as a faculty fellow, and I am grateful for the Institute's support for my work.

From start to finish, Jon Liebman of Brillstein Entertainment was a partner in thought, with constant substantive insights and indispensable process advice. The unfailingly encouraging Richard Lovett at Creative Artists Agency, along with his colleagues Kate Childs, Mollie Glick, and David Larabell, were instrumental in framing the project and guiding it toward publication.

Acknowledgments

Were it not for the trust and respect I have for Bob Weil of Liveright Publishing, this book could not have come together in time, or at all. Bob's belief in me as an author, and his uncompromising attention to the text, ensured that these thoughts and words took meaningful shape. I am grateful to him and to his colleagues at Norton, working under the leadership of chair Julia Reidhead, for a great deal, including the swift responsiveness of Gabe Kachuck, the keen copyediting of Dave Cole, and the myriad contributions of Peter Miller, Cordelia Calvert, Nick Curley, Anna Oler, Don Rifkin, Elisabeth Kerr, Steve Attardo, and Steven Pace.

Jennifer Huang, helping at every turn as she did on *Shortest Way Home*, again proved her remarkable research and analytical capacity, contributing not just well-sourced information but insightful analysis and perspective. Dylan Loewe, who became deeply involved during the final days of manuscript preparation, applied his gifts of clarity, storytelling, and political experience to make it possible for this manuscript to reach completion on time.

I am grateful to team members from Win the Era and veterans of Pete For America, including Marcus Switzer, Michael Halle, Lis Smith, Hari Sevugan, Mike Schmuhl, Katie Connolly, Larry Grisolano, and Portia Allen-Kyle, for their willingness to look at drafts and for their very helpful suggestions and critiques. And conversations with friends including Ganesh Sitaraman, Swati Mylavarapu, and Sabeel Rahman led me in important intellectual directions I would not otherwise have considered.

Acknowledgments

Most importantly, this book would have been neither conceived nor completed without the constant support of my husband, Chasten, who always senses what I need most, whether it's a new thought to explore on the page, or an afternoon away from the desk. His love, and trust, inspire me daily.

Trust and Distrust in America—A Report of the Pew Research Center[*]

BY LEE RAINIE, SCOTT KEETER, AND ANDREW PERRIN

I've devoted much of this book to my personal and political reflections and experiences, and how they have led me to pay attention to the centrality of building trust if we are to meet the major challenges we face in the decade ahead. There is excellent scientific data on the subject, including the 2019 Pew Research study "Trust and Distrust in America," which I have mentioned in the text. While the study is a snapshot in time (the survey was conducted in late 2018), it demonstrates that a majority of Americans believe that there has been a marked decline in trust in our government and in one another. At the same time, it reflects many patterns and insights that can inform efforts to restore public trust, and it confirms that many Ameri-

---

[*] "Trust and Distrust in America." Pew Research Center, Washington, D.C. (July 22, 2019) https://www.pewresearch.org/politics/2019/07/22/trust-and-distrust-in-america/

cans care about this as an issue. The data and findings in this study deserve attention from anyone concerned about the future of trust in America. With Pew's permission, I have excerpted a portion of the study here.

★ ★ ★

Many Americans think declining trust in the government and in each other makes it harder to solve key problems. They have a wealth of ideas about what's gone wrong and how to fix it.

Trust is an essential elixir for public life and neighborly relations, and when Americans think about trust these days, they worry. Two-thirds of adults think other Americans have little or no confidence in the federal government. Majorities believe the public's confidence in the U.S. government and in each other is shrinking, and most believe a shortage of trust in government and in other

Americans think their distrust of the federal government and each other is a problem that gets in the way of solving issues

% of U.S. adults who believe . . .

	The federal government	Each other
. . . Americans' trust in ____ has been shrinking	75%	64%
. . . It is very important that the U.S. improve the level of confidence Americans have in ____	68	58
. . . low trust in ____ makes it harder to solve problems	64	70

Source: Survey conducted Nov. 27–Dec. 10, 2018.
"Trust and Distrust in America"
Pew Research Center

citizens makes it harder to solve some of the nation's key problems.

As a result, many think it is necessary to clean up the trust environment: 68% say it is very important to repair the public's level of confidence in the federal government, and 58% say the same about improving confidence in fellow Americans.

Moreover, some see fading trust as a sign of cultural sickness and national decline. Some also tie it to what they perceive to be increased loneliness and excessive individualism. About half of Americans (49%) link the decline in interpersonal trust to a belief that people are not as reliable as they used to be. Many ascribe shrinking trust to a political culture they believe is broken and spawns suspicion, even cynicism, about the ability of others to distinguish fact from fiction.

In a comment typical of the views expressed by many people of different political leanings, ages and educational backgrounds, one participant in a new Pew Research Center survey said: "Many people no longer think the federal government can actually be a force for good or change in their lives. This kind of apathy and disengagement will lead to an even worse and less representative government." Another addressed the issue of fading interpersonal trust: "As a democracy founded on the principle of E Pluribus Unum, the fact that we are divided and can't trust sound facts means we have lost our confidence in each other."

Even as they express doleful views about the state of trust today, many Americans believe the situation can be turned around. Fully 84% believe the level of confidence Americans have in the federal government can be improved, and 86% think improvement is possible when it comes to the confidence Americans have in each other. Among the solutions they offer in their open-ended comments: muffle political partisanship and group-centered tribalism, refocus news coverage away from insult-ridden talk shows and sensationalist stories, stop giving so much attention to digital screens and spend more time with people, and practice empathy. Some believe their neighborhoods are a key place where interpersonal trust can be rebuilt if people work together on local projects, in turn radiating trust out to other sectors of the culture.

The new survey of 10,618 U.S. adults, conducted Nov. 27–Dec. 10, 2018, using the Center's nationally representative American Trends Panel, covers a wide range of trust-related issues and adds context to debates about the state of trust and distrust in the nation. The margin of sampling error for the full sample is plus or minus 1.5 percentage points.

In addition to asking traditional questions about whether Americans have confidence in institutions and other human beings, the survey explores links between institutional trust and interpersonal trust and examines the degree to which the public thinks the nation is shackled by these issues. This research is part of the Center's extensive and ongoing focus on issues tied to trust, facts and democracy and the interplay among them.

Here are some of the main findings.

Levels of personal trust are associated with race and ethnicity, age, education and household income. To explore these connections, we asked questions about people's general trust or distrust in others, their sense of the exploitative tendencies or fairness of others, and their assessment of the overall helpfulness or selfishness of others. Then, we

Personal trust ranges across a spectrum, with differences in levels of trust tied to race and ethnicity, age, education and household income

% of U.S. adults who fall into different trust groups

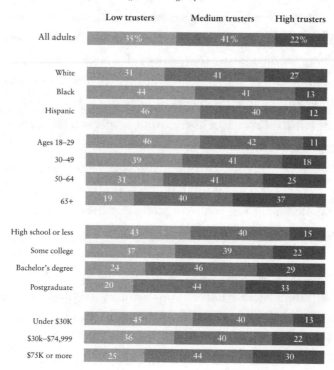

	Low trusters	Medium trusters	High trusters
All adults	35%	41%	22%
White	31	41	27
Black	44	41	13
Hispanic	46	40	12
Ages 18–29	46	42	11
30–49	39	41	18
50–64	31	41	25
65+	19	40	37
High school or less	43	40	15
Some college	37	39	22
Bachelor's degree	24	46	29
Postgraduate	20	44	33
Under $30K	45	40	13
$30k–$74,999	36	40	22
$75K or more	25	44	30

Note: Respondents who did not give an answer are not shown. The trust scale is built on questions about people's general trust or distrust in othrs, and their assessment of the overall helpfulness or selfishness of others. For details, see Chapter 2 subsection "People sort along a continuum of personal trust." White and blacks only includes non-Hispanics. Hispanics are of any race.
Source: Survey conducted Nov. 27–Dec. 10, 2018
"Trust and Distrust in America"
Pew Research Center

built a scale of personal trust and distributed people along a spectrum from least trusting to most trusting. About a fifth of adults (22%) display consistently trustful attitudes on these questions, and roughly a third (35%) express consistently wary or distrustful views. Some 41% hold mixed views on core personal trust questions.

There are some notable demographic variations in levels of personal trust, which, even in these new contexts, follow historic trends captured by the Center and other researchers. The share of whites who show high levels of trust (27%) is twice as high as the share of blacks (13%) and Hispanics (12%). The older a person is, the more likely they are to tilt toward more trustful answers. The more education Americans have, and the greater their household income, the greater the likelihood they are high on the personal trust spectrum. Those with less income and education are markedly more likely to be low trusters.

In other words, personal trust turns out to be like many other personal attributes and goods that are arrayed unequally in society, following the same overall pattern as home ownership and wealth, for example. Americans who might feel disadvantaged are less likely to express generalized trust in other people.

Strikingly, nearly half of young adults (46%) are in the low trust group—a significantly higher share than among older adults. Also, there are no noteworthy partisan differences in levels of personal trust: Republicans and Democrats distribute the same way across the scale. It is worth noting, of course, that while social trust is seen as a virtue and a societal bonding agent, too much trust can be a serious liability. Indiscriminate trusters can be victimized in any number of ways, so wariness and doubt have their place in a well-functioning community.

Levels of personal trust tend to be linked with people's broader views on institutions and civic life. The disposition of U.S. adults to trust, or not to trust, each other is connected with their thinking about all manner of issues. For instance, those who are less trusting in the interpersonal sphere also tend to be less trusting of institutions, less sure their fellow citizens will act in ways that are good for civic life and less confident that trust levels can rise in the future.

Also, Americans' views on interpersonal trust provide strong clues to how they think their fellow citizens will react in a variety of civic circumstances; their confidence in

Those with high personal trust have higher confidence in key leadership groups

% of U. S. adults in each group who have a great deal/fair amount of confidence that _____ will act in the best interests of the pblic

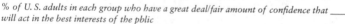

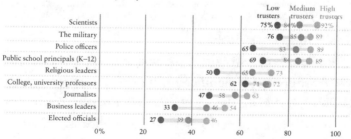

	Low trusters	Medium trusters	High trusters
Scientists	75%	84%	92%
The military	76	85	89
Police officers	65	83	89
Public school principals (K–12)	69	84	89
Religious leaders	50	65	73
College, university professors	62	71	72
Journalists	47	58	63
Business leaders	33	46	54
Elected officials	27	39	46

Note: The trust scale is built on questions about people's general trust or distrust in others; their sense of the explotative tendencies or fairness of others; and their assessment of the overall helpfulness or selfishness of others. For details, see Chapter 2 subsection "People sort along a continuum of personal trust."
Source: Survey conducted Nov. 27–Dec 10, 2019
"Trust and Distrust in Ameria"
Pew Research Center

groups ranging from the military to scientists, college professors and religious leaders; and the strategies they embrace for dealing with others. For example, low trusters are much more likely than high trusters to say that skepticism is the best mindset for most situations (63% of low trusters say this vs. 33% of high trusters). They also are more likely than high trusters to say that being self-reliant is a better choice than working together with others (33% vs. 24%).

When Americans perceive that trust in the federal government has been shrinking, they are right. Long-running surveys show that public confidence in the government fell precipitously in the 1960s and '70s, recovered somewhat in the '80s and early 2000s, and is near historic lows today. Although there is a widespread perception that trust in other people also has plummeted, whether that truly has happened is not as clear, partly because surveys have asked questions about personal trust less frequently or consistently.

By and large, Americans think the current low level of trust in government is justified. Just one-in-four (24%) say the federal government deserves more public confidence than it gets, while 75% say that it does *not* deserve any more public confidence than it gets. Similarly, among U.S. adults who perceive that confidence in each other has dropped, many think there is good reason for it: More than twice as many say Americans have lost confidence in each other "because people are not as reliable as they used to be" (49% support that statement) than take the opposite view, saying Americans have lost confidence in each other "even though people are as reliable as they have always been" (21% say that).

The trust landscape isn't entirely bleak: Most Americans have confidence others will uphold key civic virtues, though not in every case. Clear majorities of Americans are confident their fellow citizens will act in a number of important pro-civic ways. This includes reporting serious local problems to authorities, obeying federal and state laws, doing what they can to help those in need and honestly reporting their income when paying taxes.

However, this level of confidence does not extend across all civic activities. It seems to plunge as soon as politics enter the picture. U.S. adults render a split verdict on whether they can count on fellow Americans to accept election results regardless of who wins: 53% express "a fair amount" or "a great deal" of confidence that others will accept the results, while 47% say they have "not too much" or "no confidence at all" that others will accept the election outcome. Americans also are split on whether they can rely on others to reconsider their views after learning new information (49% have at least some confidence, 50% little or none), stay informed about important issues and events (49% vs. 51%) and respect the rights of people who are not like them (48% vs. 52%).

Moreover, in some areas Americans do *not* expect others to act in civically helpful ways. Some 58% of adults are not confident that others can hold civil conversations with people who have different views, and 57% are not

Appendix One

Many Americans have confidence in others to do the right thing in civic life at times, but not always

% of U.S. adults who have _____ in the American people to . . .

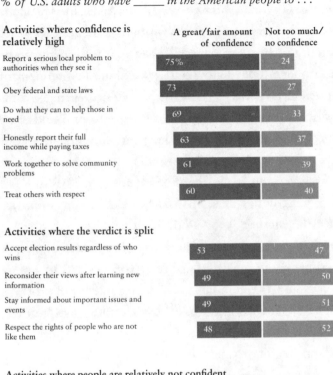

Activities where confidence is relatively high

	A great/fair amount of confidence	Not too much/ no confidence
Report a serious local problem to authorities when they see it	75%	24
Obey federal and state laws	73	27
Do what they can to help those in need	69	33
Honestly report their full income while paying taxes	63	37
Work together to solve community problems	61	39
Treat others with respect	60	40

Activities where the verdict is split

Accept election results regardless of who wins	53	47
Reconsider their views after learning new information	49	50
Stay informed about important issues and events	49	51
Respect the rights of people who are not like them	48	52

Activities where people are relatively not confident

Cast informed votes in elections	43	57
Have civil conversations with people who have different views from theirs	42	58

Note: Respondents who did not give an answer are not shown.
Source: Survey conducted Nov. 27–Dec. 10, 2018.
"Trust and Distrust in America"
Pew Research Center

194

confident others will cast informed votes in elections. One notable pro-trust finding is that, at least in principle, more adults embrace collaboration than individualism. Asked about the best way to navigate life, 71% say it is better in most situations for people to work together with others, compared with 29% who say it is better to be self-reliant. Additionally, the inclination of Americans to express different levels of trust depending on the circumstances is reflected in their views on various institutions and kinds of leaders. The military enjoys "a great deal" or "fair amount" of confidence among 83% of U.S. adults, as do scientists (83%). Not far behind are principals of K–12 public schools (80%) and police officers (78%).* Confidence in journalists stands at 55%.†

These supportive views stand in contrast to the public's overall lack of confidence in elected officials and corporate leaders: 63% express little confidence in elected officials, and 56% take a similarly skeptical view of business leaders.

---

* This survey asked two questions related to public school leaders: one about the public's confidence in principals and superintendents for K–12 schools, the other just about principals (not referencing superintendents). Some 77% of respondents say they have a great deal/fair amount of confidence in public school principals and superintendents. The findings cited throughout this report are from the question focused only on principals.

† This survey asked two questions related to journalism: one about the public's confidence in journalists, the other about confidence in "the news media." Some 48% of respondents say they have a great deal/fair amount of confidence in the news media. The findings cited throughout this report are from the question about journalists.

Appendix One

Democrats and Republicans think differently about trust, but both groups wish it would rise. Although supporters of the country's two main political parties hold similar levels of personal trust, Democrats and those who lean Democratic are more likely than Republicans and Republican leaners to express worry about the state of trust in America. For example, Democratic partisans are more likely to say that trust in the federal government is shrinking (82% vs. 66%) and that low trust in the federal government makes it harder to solve many of the country's problems (70% vs. 57%).

At the same time, there is bipartisan agreement that it is important to improve trust in both the federal government and in fellow Americans, as well as that there are ways to do so. There are some partisan differences, too, when it comes to confidence in Americans to act in some civically beneficial ways. For instance, 76% of Republicans and 63% of Democrats (including independents who lean toward each party) have confidence people would do what they can to help those in need. Similarly, 56% of Republicans and 42% of Democrats have confidence the American people respect the rights of people who are not like them.

Partisan differences also show up in the levels of trust extended toward various kinds of leaders, including the military, religious leaders and business leaders (groups toward whom Republicans are more favorable than Democrats) as well as scientists, public school principals, college professors and journalists (groups that generally enjoy more confidence among Democrats than among Republicans).

There is a generation gap in levels of trust. Young adults are much more pessimistic than older adults about some trust issues. For example, young adults are about half as hopeful as their elders when they are asked how confident they are in the American people to respect the rights of those who are not like them: About one-third (35%) of those ages 18 to 29 are confident Americans have that respect, compared with two-thirds (67%) of those 65 and older.

There is also a gap when it comes to confidence that Americans will do what they can to help others in need. More than four-in-ten young adults (44%) are confident the American people will accept election results no matter who wins, compared with 66% of older adults who believe that's the case.

At the same time, older Americans are more likely to believe Americans have lost confidence in each other because people are not as reliable as they used to be: 54% of those ages 65 and older take this position, compared with 44% of those 18 to 29.

Majorities believe the federal government and news media withhold important and useful information. And notable numbers say they struggle to know what's true or not when listening to elected officials. People's confidence in key institutions is associated with their views about how those institutions handle important information. About two-thirds (69%) of Americans say the federal government intentionally withholds important information from the public that it could safely release, and about six-in-ten (61%) say the news media intentionally ignores stories that

Appendix One

In some key areas, Democrats tend to worry more about trust-related issues, but members in both parties agree it is important to improve the situation

% of U.S. adults in each group who believe . . .

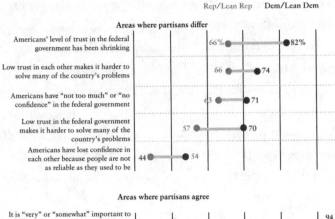

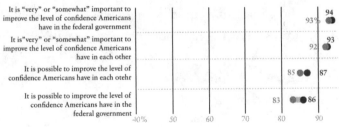

Source: Survey conducted Nov. 27–Dec. 10, 2018
"Trust and Distrust in America"
Pew Research Center

are important to the public. Those who hold these views that information is being withheld are more likely than others to have greater concerns about the state of trust.

Significant shares also assert they face challenges separating the truth from false information when they are listening to elected officials and using social media. Some 64% say it is hard to tell the difference between what is true and not true when they hear elected officials; 48% say the same thing about information they encounter on social media.

On a grand scale of national issues, trust-related issues are not near the top of the list of Americans' concerns. But people link distrust to the major problems they see, such as concerns about ethics in government and the role of lobbyists and special interests. The Center has asked questions in multiple surveys about how Americans judge the severity of some key issues. This poll finds that 41% of adults think the public's level of confidence in the federal government is a "very big problem," putting it roughly on par with their assessment of the size of the problems caused by racism and illegal immigration—and above terrorism and sexism. Some 25% say Americans' level of con-

Nearly two-thirds of adults find if hard to tell what's true when elected officials speak

% of U.S. adults who say it is ____ to tell the difference between what's true and what's not true when . . . .

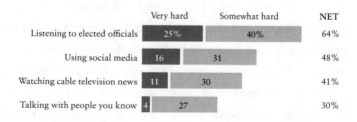

	Very hard	Somewhat hard	NET
Listening to elected officials	25%	40%	64%
Using social media	16	31	48%
Watching cable television news	11	30	41%
Talking with people you know	4	27	30%

Note: Figures may not ad up due to roundng. Respondents who gave other answers or no answer are not shown.
Source: Survey conducted Nov. 27–Dec. 10, 2018
"Trust and Distrust in America"
Pew Research Center

fidence in each other is a very big problem, which is low in comparison with a broad array of other issues that Americans perceive as major problems.

It is important to note, though, that some Americans see distrust as a factor inciting or amplifying other issues they consider crucial. For example, in their open-ended written answers to questions, numbers of Americans say they think there are direct connections between rising distrust and other trends they perceived as major problems, such as partisan paralysis in government, the outsize influence of lobbyists and moneyed interests, confusion arising from made-up news and information, declining ethics in government, the intractability of immigration and climate debates, rising health care costs and a widening gap between the rich and the poor.

Many of the answers in the open-ended written responses reflect judgments similar to this one from a 38-year-old man: "Trust is the glue that binds humans together. Without it, we cooperate with one another less, and variables in our overall quality of life are affected (e.g., health and life satisfaction)."

Americans offer a range of insights about what has happened to trust, the consequences of distrust and how to repair these problems. The open-ended survey questions invited respondents to write, in their own words, why they think trust in the U.S. government and in fellow Americans has eroded, what impact rising distrust has on government performance and personal relations, and whether there are ways trust might be restored. Some of the main findings:

Appendix One

Why trust in the federal government has deteriorated in the past generation: Some 76% of Americans believe trust in the federal government has declined in the past 20 years. When asked what happened, the respondents to this question offer a wide range of diagnoses, some of which are more commonly cited by Republicans, others of which are Democrat-dominated. Overall, 36% cite something related to how the U.S. government is performing— whether it is doing too much, too little, the wrong things or nothing at all—including how money has corrupted it, how corporations control it and general references to "the swamp." President Donald Trump and his administration are cited in 14% of answers, and the performance of the news media comes up in 10% of responses. Additionally, 9% of these respondents say distrust in government arises from big social forces that have swept the culture, such as rising inequality and the spread of individualism. Others mention the intractability of problems like climate change or illegal immigration, as well as increasing polarization among the public and its leaders.

Republicans and those who lean Republican are more likely than Democrats and those who lean that way to mention government performance problems and corruption (31% vs. 24%). But Democrats are more likely to cite Trump's performance as a contributor to problems related to trust in the federal government (24% vs. 3%).

ILLUSTRATIVE ANSWER: *"People are jaded in this day and age. Elected officials cannot be trusted. There is a huge divide between Democrats and Republicans.*

Social media allows people to air dirty laundry. People
are not as friendly and neighborly as they were years
ago. Society has drastically changed!" Woman, 46

Why Americans' trust in each other has deteriorated in the
past 20 years: Some 71% think that interpersonal trust has
declined. Those who take this position were asked why,
eliciting a laundry list of societal and political problems:
11% believe Americans on the whole have become more
lazy, greedy and dishonest. Some 16% of respondents make
a connection between what they think is poor government
performance—especially gridlock in Washington—and
the toll it has taken on their fellow citizens' hearts. About
one-in-ten of these respondents say they blame the news
media and its focus on divisive and sensational coverage.

ILLUSTRATIVE ANSWER: *"Cultural shift away from*
close-knit communities. Viewing everything through
hyperpartisan political lenses. Lost the art of com-
promise. Empathy as well as generally attempting to
understand and to help each other are all at disturb-
ingly low levels. People are quick to attack and to vil-
ify others, even without clear proof, solely on the basis
of accusations or along partisan lines." Man, 44

What would improve the public's level of confidence in
the federal government: Some 84% of Americans believe
it is possible to improve the level of confidence people have
in the government. Their written responses urge various

political reforms, starting with more disclosure of what the government is doing, as well as term limits and restrictions on the role of money in politics. Some 15% of those who answered this question point to a need for better political leadership, including greater honesty and cooperation among those in the political class. A small share believes confidence will rise when Trump is out of office. Additionally, some offer specific roadmaps for rebuilding trust, often starting with local community-based solutions that rise upward to regional and national levels.

ILLUSTRATIVE ANSWER: *"1. If members of each party would be less concerned about their power and the next election and more concerned with how they can serve their people. Term limits a possibility. 2. Rules about lobbyists/corporate money influencing politicians. 3. Importance of ethics laws and follow through for violators. 4. Promoting fact-based legislation. 5. Better relations among both parties and leaders; this is not a war." Woman, 63*

What would improve Americans' level of confidence in each other: Fully 86% believe it is possible to improve interpersonal confidence across the nation, and a number of their answers focus on how local communities can be laboratories for trust-building to confront partisan tensions and overcome tribal divisions. One-in-ten make the case that better leaders could inspire greater trust between individuals. Some suggest that a different approach to news reporting—one that emphasizes the ways people cooperate to solve problems—would have a tonic effect.

> ILLUSTRATIVE ANSWER: *"Get to know your local community. Take small steps towards improving daily life, even if it's just a trash pick-up. If people feel engaged with their environment and with each other, and they can work together even in a small way, I think that builds a foundation for working together on more weighty issues."* Woman, 32

Why Americans' low public confidence in each other and in the federal government is a "very big" problem: Some 25% think this, and the majority of those who explain their views cite their distress over broad social issues, including the shriveling trust neighbors have in each other, the toll political partisanship and tribalism take on interpersonal relations, a rise in selfishness, or a decline in civility and moral behavior. Some mention political leaders.

> ILLUSTRATIVE ANSWER: *"Everything is impacted by the lack of trust—and the driver of the declining trust is the head of the federal government. Trust cannot be repaired without truth—which is in short supply."* Woman, 56

The issues that cannot be effectively addressed because Americans do not trust the federal government: Nearly two-thirds (64%) say that low trust in the federal government makes it harder to solve many of the country's problems. About four-in-ten of those who then give follow-up answers (39%) cite social issues topped by issues in immigration and the border, health care and insurance, racism and race relations, or guns and gun violence. Some also cite environmental issues, tax and budget matters, or political processes like voting rights and gerrymandering.

ILLUSTRATIVE ANSWER: *"The *entire* general functioning of society. Trust in the federal government is low due to, in my opinion, unqualified people running it who are often dishonest. When you can't trust elected and appointed officials, it impedes essentially everything in the government's purview from working properly." Man, 30*

Closing Address of the 2020 Pete Buttigieg Campaign for President

Address to supporters on ending the campaign

IT'S SO GOOD TO BE IN SOUTH BEND. SOMETIMES the longest way around really is the shortest way home. Here we are. In the last few years, America has faced enormous challenges, from an economy in transition, to a climate on the brink, to a president sowing chaos and discord across the very country he is responsible for uniting. And for many Americans, these challenges have amounted to a call to action. And so, like so many others, I thought deeply about what I could do to make a difference, what I could do to make myself useful. And it was in that spirit, with your help, that a year ago we launched our campaign for the American presidency. We began this unlikely journey with a staff of four in a cramped office right here in South Bend, Indiana, right down Washington Street. No big email list. No personal fortune. Hardly anybody knew my name and even fewer could pronounce it, but South Bend showed everybody what to do. First name Mayor, last name Pete, so nobody got confused.

But by every conventional wisdom, by every historical measure, we were never supposed to get anywhere at all. And then, as I said, that roller-coaster February night a few weeks ago, when Iowa shocked the nation, along that way, an improbable hope became an undeniable reality.

In a field in which more than two dozen Democratic candidates ran for president, senators and governors, billionaires, a former vice president, we achieved a top-four finish in each of the first four states to hold nominating contests, and we made history winning those Iowa caucuses.

And all of that, it came about thanks to your support. Thanks to the power of this campaign's vision in your hands. It proved that Americans really are hungry for a new kind of politics, rooted in the values that we share. In cities and suburbs, in rural communities, in crowds that spilled out of venues from Salt Lake City, to Raleigh, to Arlington, we saw Americans ready to meet a new era of challenge with a new generation of leadership. We found countless Americans ready to support a middle-class Millennial mayor from the industrial Midwest, not in spite of that experience, but because of it, eager to get Washington to start working like our best-run communities and towns.

In a divided nation, we saw fellow Democrats join with independents and, yes, some of those future former Republicans, to choose a different politics, to choose a politics defined not by who we push away, but by how many we can call to our side.

And we sent a message to every kid out there wondering if whatever marks them out as different means they are somehow destined to be less than, to see that someone who once felt that exact same way can become a leading American presidential candidate with his husband at his side.

We got into this race for a reason. We got into this race in order to defeat the current president and in order to usher in a new kind of politics. And that meant guiding our campaign by the values we like to call the rules of the road. Respect, belonging, truth, teamwork, boldness, responsibility, substance, discipline, excellence, and joy. And every decision we made was guided by these values.

One of those values is truth. And today is a moment of truth. After a year of going everywhere, meeting everyone, defying every expectation, seeking every vote, the truth is that the path has narrowed to a close for our candidacy, if not for our cause.

And another of those values is responsibility. And we have a responsibility to consider the effect of remaining in this race any further. Our goal has always been to help unify Americans to defeat Donald Trump and to win the era for our values. And so we must recognize that at this point in the race, the best way to keep faith with those goals and ideals is to step aside and help bring our party and our country together.

So tonight I am making the difficult decision to suspend my campaign for the presidency. I will no longer seek to be the 2020 Democratic nominee for president, but I will do everything in my power to ensure that we have a new Democratic president come January.

We have to, because every time this president brings partisan politics into the management of a deadly serious pandemic, or purges officials who honored their oaths of office by telling the truth, or cloaks in religious language an administration whose actions harm the least among us, the sick and the poor, the outcast and the stranger, we are reminded just how urgent it is that we change who is in the White House. We cannot afford to miss this moment.

With every passing day, I am more and more convinced that the only way we will defeat Trump and Trumpism is with a new politics that gathers people together. We need leadership to heal a divided nation, not drive us further apart. We need a broad-based agenda that can truly deliver for the American people, not one that gets lost in ideology. We need an approach strong enough not only to win the White House, but to hold the House, win the Senate, and send Mitch McConnell into retirement.

And that broad and inclusive politics, that is the politics that we've attempted to model through this campaign that I believe is the way forward for our eventual nominee. So I urge everyone who supported me to continue in the cause of ensuring that we bring change to the White House and working to win the absolutely critical down-ballot races playing out across the country this year.

There is simply too much at stake to retreat to the sidelines at a time like this. As this contest gives way to the season of weekly elections and delegate math, it is more important than ever that we hold to what this is actually all about. Politics is not about the horse race, not about the debate stage, or a precinct count in a spreadsheet. It is about real people's lives. It is about our paychecks, our families, our futures. We can and must put the everyday lives of Americans who have been overlooked for so long back at the center of our politics, and every story that became part of this campaign helped show us why and how we do just that.

Politics is about people, and that is especially true of the people who touched this campaign. To my competitors in a historically diverse field, those who have stepped aside and those still competing, thank you for demonstrating what public service can be.

To the people of South Bend, this river city we love so much: thank you for keeping me honest and thank you for keeping me going. And to our Pete for America family, I cannot express how grateful I am to every staffer, every volunteer, every supporter who believed in what we were building.

You walked in neighborhoods on hot summer days and drove on icy roads in the wintertime, you filmed and tweeted and coded and crunched numbers. You built relationships and you built events. You lit up offices and you filled high school gyms with equipment and then with people and then with cheers, in the name of our values, freedom and security and democracy.

Our contributors, so many of you dug deep to fuel this campaign. Nearly a million grassroots supporters who sacrificed financially so that this message of hope and belonging could reach every corner of this country. Thank you for what you gave to make this possible.

Online, in person, with family and with friends and with total strangers, you shared your personal stories and you made the life of this campaign part of your own. What you did and the way you did it was how we could show, not just tell, the kind of campaign we could be and the kind of country we will build. You made me proud every single day.

And last, I want to thank my own family. My mom, who not only helped raise me but put her love of language into work answering letters for the campaign. My father, who left us just as this was all getting under way, but he was very much here and part of this effort. And to the guy who took a chance on a first date with somebody all the way in South Bend, Indiana, and never looked back. Chasten, I can't wait to spend the rest of my life with you.

I know that as this campaign ends, there comes disappointment that we won't continue, but I hope that everyone who has been part of this in any way knows that the campaign that you have built and the community that you have created is only the beginning of the change that we are going to make together.

My faith teaches that the world is not divided into good people and bad people, that all of us are capable of good and bad things. Today, more than ever, politics matters because leaders can call out either what is best in us or what is worst in us, can draw us either to our better or to our worst selves. Politics at its worst is ugly, but at its best politics can lift us up. It is not just policy making, it is moral. It is soul craft. That is why we were in this.

Earlier today, we were in Selma marching in commemoration of the civil rights movement on the Edmund Pettus

Bridge, where I was humbled to walk in the symbolic and the literal shadows of heroes who fifty-five years ago made America more of a democracy than it had ever been by their blood and by their courage. And seeing those moral giants made me ask what we might achieve in the years now at hand, how we might live up to the greatest moral traditions of political change in this country. It made me wonder how the 2020s will be remembered when I am an old man.

I firmly believe that in these years, in our time, we can and will make American life and politics more like what they could be, not just more wise and more prosperous, but more equitable, and more just, and more decent.

Think of how proud of our time we could be if we really did act to make it so that no one has to take to the streets in America for a decent wage because one job is enough in the United States of America, whether you went to college or not.

Imagine how proud we would be to be the generation that saw the day when your race has no bearing on your health, or your wealth, or your relationship with law enforcement in the United States.

What if we could be the ones to deliver the day when our teachers are honored a little more like soldiers and paid a little more like doctors?

What if we were the ones who rallied this nation to see to it that climate would be no barrier to our children's opportunities in life?

The chance to do that is in our hands. That is the hope in

our hearts. That is the fire in our bellies. That is the future we believe in. A country that really does empower every American to thrive and a future where everyone belongs.

Thank you for sharing that vision. Thank you for helping us spread that hope. Thank you so much. Let's move on together. Thank you.

March 1, 2020
South Bend, Indiana

Notes

CHAPTER ONE

The Necessity of Trust

1. Dincer, Oguzhan C., and Eric M. Uslaner. "Trust
   and Growth." *Public Choice* 142 (2010): 59–67. doi
   .org/10.1007/s11127-009-9473-4.
2. El-Qorchi, Mohammed, Samuel Munzele Maimbo, and
   John F. Wilson. "Informal Funds Transfer Systems: An
   Analysis of the Informal Hawala System." IMF Occasional Paper no. 222. Washington, D.C.: International
   Monetary Fund, 2003.
3. Zimmerman, Laura. "Deception Detection." *Monitor
   on Psychology* 47, no. 3 (2016): 46.
4. Lewis, John, and Michael D'Orso. *Walking with the
   Wind: A Memoir of the Movement.* New York: Simon
   & Schuster, 1998.
5. Bertrand, Marianne, and Sendhil Mullainathan. "Are
   Emily and Greg More Employable Than Lakisha and
   Jamal? A Field Experiment on Labor Market Discrimination." *American Economic Review* 94, no. 4 (2004):
   991–1013. doi.org/10.1257/0002828042002561.
6. Faber, Jacob William, and Terri Friedline. *The Racial-*

ized Costs of Banking. Washington, D.C.: New America, 2018. https://www.newamerica.org/family-centered
-social-policy/reports/racialized-costs-banking/.

7. Federal Deposit Insurance Corporation. *2017 FDIC
    National Survey of Unbanked and Underbanked House-
    holds,* by Gerald Apaam, et al. Washington, D.C., 2018.
    https://www.fdic.gov/householdsurvey/2017/2017report
    .pdf.

CHAPTER TWO

The Loss of Trust

1. Mendes, Elizabeth. "The Study That Helped Spur the
    U.S. Stop-Smoking Movement." *American Cancer Soci-
    ety,* January 9, 2014. https://www.cancer.org.
2. "Smoking and Health Proposal." Brown & William-
    son Records; Minnesota Documents; Tobacco Industry
    Influence in Public Policy; Master Settlement Agree-
    ment. 1969. https://www.industrydocuments.ucsf.edu/
    docs/psdw0147.
3. "Public Trust in Government Remains Near Historic
    Lows as Partisan Attitudes Shift." Washington, D.C.:
    Pew Research Center, 2017.
4. Saad, Lydia. "Military, Small Business, Police Still Stir
    Most Confidence." Washington, D.C.: Gallup Organiza-
    tion, 2018.
5. Rainie, Lee, Scott Keeter, and Andrew Perrin. "Trust
    and Distrust in America." Washington, D.C.: Pew
    Research Center, 2019.

6. Smith, Tom W., Michael Davern, Jeremy Freese, and Stephen Morgan. *General Social Surveys, 1972–2018 [machine-readable data file]*. Chicago: NORC at the University of Chicago, 2018. gssdataexplorer.norc.org.

7. Jamieson, Dave. "This Is What It's Like to Sit Through an Anti-Union Meeting At Work." *Huffington Post*, September 3, 2014. https://www.huffpost.com.

8. Katz, Jon. "Birth of a Digital Nation." *Wired*, April 1, 1997. https://www.wired.com/1997/04/netizen-3/.

9. Trippi, Joe. *The Revolution Will Not Be Televised*. New York: ReganBooks, 2005.

10. Anderson, Robert H., Christopher Kedzie, Tora K. Bikson, Brent R. Keltner, Sally Ann Law, Constantijn (Stan) Panis, Bridger M. Mitchell, Joel Pliskin, and Padmanabhan Srinagesh. *Universal Access to E-Mail: Feasibility and Societal Implications*. Santa Monica, CA: RAND Corporation, 1995.

11. "Partisan Conflict and Congressional Outreach." Washington, D.C.: Pew Research Center, 2017.

12. Blake, Aaron. "A New Study Suggests Fake News Might Have Won Donald Trump the 2016 Election." *Washington Post*, April 3, 2018. https://www.washingtonpost.com.

13. Hendrickson, Clara. "Local Journalism in Crisis: Why America Must Revive Its Local Newsrooms." Washington, D.C.: Brookings Institution, 2019.

14. Broniatowski, David A., Amelia M. Jamison, SiHua Qi, Lulwah AlKulaib, Tao Chen, Adrian Benton, Sandra C. Quinn, and Mark Dredze. "Weaponized Health Communication: Twitter Bots and Russian Trolls Amplify the Vaccine Debate." *American Journal of Public*

Health 108, no. 10 (2018): 1378–1384. doi.org/10.2105/
AJPH.2018.304567.

15. Howard, Philip N., Bharath Ganesh, Dimitra Liot-
siou, John Kelly, and Camille François. "The IRA,
Social Media and Political Polarization in the United
States, 2012–2018." Oxford: University of Oxford,
2018. https://comprop.oii.ox.ac.uk/research/ira-political
-polarization/.

16. "The Senate Intelligence Committee Report on Russian
Active Measures Campaigns and Interference in the 2016
U.S. Election. Volume 2: Russia's Use of Social Media
with Additional Views." 116th Congress 1st Session Senate Report 116-XX.

17. Lenz, Lyz. "The Iowa Caucus Wasn't 'Rigged' by an App
to Help Pete Buttigieg. Democracy Is Just Messy." *NBC
News*, February 5, 2020. https://www.nbcnews.com.

18. Perlroth, Nicole. "A Conspiracy Made in America May
Have Been Spread by Russia." *New York Times*, June
15, 2020. https://www.nytimes.com.

19. American News Pathways data tool. "% of Each Group
Who Say the Release of the Results of the Iowa Demo-
cratic Caucus Was Delayed Because . . ." Washington,
D.C.: Pew Research Center, 2020.

20. Frankfurter, Felix. *The Public and Its Government*. New
Haven, CT: Yale University Press, 1930. Quoted in Jill
Lepore, *These Truths* (New York: W.W. Norton, 2018).

21. Shepard, Walter J. "Democracy in Transition." *The
American Political Science Review* 29, no. 1 (1935):
1–20.

CHAPTER THREE
Trust for a Deciding Decade

1. Booth, William, Carolyn Y. Johnson, and Carol Morello. "The World Came Together for a Virtual Vaccine Summit. The U.S. Was Conspicuously Absent." *Washington Post*, May 4, 2020. https://www.washingtonpost.com.

2. Yahoo News / YouGov. "Yahoo! News Coronavirus—May 22, 2020."

3. Associated Press / NORC Center for Public Affairs Research at the University of Chicago. "Expectations for a COVID-19 Vaccine." Chicago: NORC at the University of Chicago, 2020.

4. Morning Consult / Politico. "National Tracking Poll #200386—March 20–22, 2020." Washington, D.C.: Morning Consult, 2020.

5. CBS News / YouGov. "CBS News Poll—May 11–13, 2020."

6. Axelrod, Tal. "Fauci: 'I Think You Can Trust Me' on My Track Record." *The Hill*, July 14, 2020. https://thehill.com.

7. Mitchell, Amy, J. Mark Jurkowitz, J. Baxter Oliphant, and Elisa Shearer. "Three Months In, Many Americans See Exaggeration, Conspiracy Theories and Partisanship in COVID-19 News." Washington, D.C.: Pew Research Center, 2020.

8. Falk, Armin, Anke Becker, Thomas Dohmen, Benjamin Enke, David Huffman, and Uwe Sunde. "Global

Evidence on Economic Preferences." *Quarterly Journal of Economics* 133, no. 4 (2018): 1645–1692. doi .org/10.1093/qje/qjy013.

9. Sprunt, Barbara, and Alana Wise. "Trump Addresses Tightly Packed Arizona Crowd Amid State's Growing Coronavirus Crisis." NPR, June 23, 2020. https://www .npr.org.

10. Cohen, Elizabeth. "Fauci Says Covid-19 Vaccine May Not Get U.S. to Herd Immunity If Too Many People Refuse to Get It." CNN, June 28, 2020. https://www.cnn.com.

11. C-SPAN. *COVID-19 Response and Reopening Schools [Video file].* June 30, 2020. https://www.c-span.org/ video/?473393-1/covid-19-response-reopening-schools.

12. Gür, Nurullah. "Does Social Trust Promote Behaviour Aimed at Mitigating Climate Change?" *Economic Affairs* 40, no. 1 (2020): 36–49. doi.org/10.1111/ ecaf.12384. Smith, E. Keith, and Adam Mayer. "A Social Trap for the Climate? Collective Action, Trust and Climate Change Risk Perception in 35 Countries." *Global Environmental Change* 49 (2018): 140–153. doi .org/10.1016/j.gloenvcha.2018.02.014.

13. Funk, Cary, and Brian Kennedy. "The Politics of Climate." Washington, D.C.: Pew Research Center, 2016.

14. Masson-Delmotte, Valerie, et al. "Global Warming of 1.5°C." Geneva, Switzerland: Intergovernmental Panel on Climate Change, 2018.

15. Rubin, James P. "Stumbling into War." *Foreign Affairs* 82, no. 5 (2003): 46–66.

16. Wike, Richard, Jacob Poushter, and Hani Zainulbhai. "As Obama Years Draw to Close, President and U.S.

Seen Favorably in Europe and Asia." Washington, D.C.: Pew Research Center, 2016.

17. Broad, William J. "Putin's Long War Against American Science." *New York Times*, April 13, 2020. https://www.nytimes.com.

18. Zhongyuan, Zhang. "Belt and Road Initiative by No Means a Debt Trap." *China Daily*, March 28, 2019. https://www.chinadaily.com.cn.

19. "Trust Is the Foundation for Belt and Road Cooperation: China Daily Editorial." *China Daily*, April 29, 2019. https://www.chinadaily.com.cn

20. Drew, Kevin. "U.S. Suffers Greatest Global Decline in Trust." *U.S. News & World Report*, January 15, 2020. https://www.usnews.com.

21. Jefferson, Thomas. "From Thomas Jefferson to David Hartley, 2 July 1787." *Founders Online*, National Archives. https://founders.archives.gov/documents/Jefferson/01-11-02-0441.

22. Burke, Edmund. *Reflections on the Revolution in France*. London: J. Dodsley, 1790.

23. Adams, John. "[Notes for an Oration at Braintree, Spring 1772.]." *Founders Online*, National Archives. https://founders.archives.gov/documents/Adams/01-02-02-0002-0002-0001.

24. Jefferson, Thomas. "Proposals to Revise the Virginia Constitution: I. Thomas Jefferson to 'Henry Tompkinson' (Samuel Kercheval), 12 July 1816." *Founders Online*, National Archives. https://founders.archives.gov/documents/Jefferson/03-10-02-0128-0002.

25. Lincoln, Abraham. *Abraham Lincoln Papers: Series 3.*

Notes

General Correspondence. 1837 to 1897: Abraham Lincoln, Tuesday, Memorandum on Probable Failure of Reelection; Endorsed by Members of Cabinet. 1864. https://www.loc.gov/item/mal4359700/.

CHAPTER FOUR
Rebuilding Trust

1. Saad, Lydia. "Concerns About Sexual Harassment Higher Than in 1998." Washington, D.C.: Gallup Organization, 2017.
2. Valenti, Jessica. "Why 'Trust' Is the Word of the Year." *Medium*, December 13, 2018. https://medium.com.
3. Klein, Ezra. *Why We're Polarized*. New York: Avid Readers Press / Simon & Schuster, 2020.
4. Silver, Nate. "Only 20 Percent of Voters Are 'Real Americans.'" *FiveThirtyEight*, July 21, 2016. https://fivethirtyeight.com.
5. United Nations Development Program. "Human Development Data (1990–2018): Life Expectancy at Birth (Years)." http://hdr.undp.org/en/data. World Health Organization. "Global Health Observatory (GHO) Data: Life Expectancy." https://www.who.int/gho/mortality_burden_disease/life_tables/en/.
6. United Nations Development Program. "Human Development Data (1990–2018): Maternal mortality ratio (deaths per 100,000 live births)." http://hdr.undp.org/en/data.
7. Organisation for Economic Cooperation and Develop-

ment. "Enrolment Rate by Age." https://stats.oecd.org/Index.aspx?DataSetCode=EAG_ENRL_RATE_AGE.

8. Helliwell, John F., Richard Layard, Jeffrey Sachs, and Jan-Emmanuel De Neve, eds. *World Happiness Report 2020.* New York: Sustainable Development Solutions Network, 2020.

9. Organisation for Economic Cooperation and Development. *A Broken Social Elevator? How to Promote Social Mobility.* Paris: OECD Publishing, 2018. doi .org/10.1787/9789264301085-en.

10. Arendt, Hannah. "Lying in Politics," in *Crisis of the Republic.* New York: Harcourt Brace Jovanovich, 1972.

11. CBC Radio. "Residential School Survivors' Stories Motivated People to Make Canada Better, says Murray Sinclair." Canadian Broadcasting Corporation, December 4, 2018. https://www.cbc.ca.

12. Baker, Kevin. "Nothing in All Creation Is Hidden." *New Republic*, May 17, 2018. https://newrepublic.com.

13. Moyer, Justin Wm. "Exactly the Right Words, Exactly the Right Way: Reagan's Amazing Challenger Disaster Speech." *Washington Post*, January 28, 2016. https://www.washingtonpost.com.

About the Author

PETE BUTTIGIEG served as mayor of the city of South Bend, Indiana, for two terms, from 2012 through 2019.

He sought the 2020 Democratic nomination for the presidency, emerging among the top candidates in a field of over two dozen before withdrawing from the race in March of 2020. He won the Iowa Democratic Caucuses, becoming the first openly LGBTQ candidate to win a state presidential nominating contest.

Born in 1982, Buttigieg grew up in South Bend and attended Saint Joseph's High School there. He attended Harvard, earning a bachelor's degree in history and literature, and went on to study philosophy, politics, and economics at Pembroke College, Oxford, as a Rhodes Scholar.

An officer in the U.S. Navy Reserve from 2009 to 2017, Buttigieg took a leave of absence to serve in Afghanistan during a seven-month deployment in 2014, earning the Joint Service Commendation Medal for his counterterrorism work.

An active musician, Buttigieg plays piano and guitar, and has performed with the South Bend Symphony Orchestra. He lives in South Bend with his husband, Chasten Buttigieg, and their dogs, Truman and Buddy.